Parenting Adopted Teenagers

Also published in association with Adoptionplus

for parents

Preparing for Adoption
Everything Adopting Parents Need to Know About
Preparations, Introductions and the First Few Weeks
Julia Davis
ISBN 978 1 84905 456 0
eISBN 978 0 85700 831 2

for professionals

Assessing Adoptive and Foster Parents
Improving Analysis and Understanding of Parenting Capacity
Edited by Joanne Alper and David Howe
Foreword by Dr. John Simmonds
ISBN 978 1 84905 506 2
eISBN 978 0 85700 915 9

Facilitating Meaningful Contact in
Adoption and Fostering
A Trauma-Informed Approach to Planning,
Assessing and Good Practice
Louis Sydney, Elsie Price and Adoptionplus
ISBN 978 1 84905 508 6
eISBN 978 0 85700 924 1

of related interest

Keeping Your Adoptive Family Strong
Strategies for Success
Gregory C. Keck and L. Gianforte
Foreword by Rita L. Soronen
ISBN 978 1 84905 784 4
eISBN 978 1 78450 028 3

The Unofficial Guide to Adoptive Parenting
The Small Stuff, The Big Stuff and The Stuff In Between
Sally Donovan
Foreword by Dr. Vivien Norris
Foreword by Jim Clifford OBE and Sue Clifford
ISBN 978 1 84905 536 9
eISBN 978 0 85700 959 3

Why Can't My Child Behave?
Empathic Parenting Strategies that
Work for Adoptive and Foster Families
Amber Elliott
ISBN 978 1 84905 339 6
eISBN 978 0 85700 671 4

Next Steps in Parenting the Child Who Hurts
Tykes and Teens
Caroline Archer
ISBN 978 1 85302 802 1
eISBN 978 1 84642 204 1

Parenting Adopted Teenagers

Advice for the Adolescent Years

Rachel Staff

Foreword by Hugh Thornbery

Jessica Kingsley *Publishers*
London and Philadelphia

First published in 2016
by Jessica Kingsley Publishers
73 Collier Street
London N1 9BE, UK
and
400 Market Street, Suite 400
Philadelphia, PA 19106, USA

www.jkp.com

Library of Congress Cataloging in Publication Data
Staff, Rachel.
Parenting adopted teenagers : advice for the adolescent years / Rachel Staff.
    pages cm
Includes bibliographical references and index.
    ISBN 978-1-84905-604-5 (alk. paper)
 1. Adopted children. 2. Parent and teenager. 3. Adolescence. I. Title.
        HV875.S676 2015
        649'.145--dc23
                        2015024054

British Library Cataloguing in Publication Data
A CIP catalogue record for this book is available from the British Library

ISBN 978 1 84905 604 5
eISBN 978 1 78450 069 6

Printed and bound in the United States

For Mum and for Lily x

Contents

Chapter Nine – Parents Come First:
The Importance of Support for Parents 215

Conclusion 236

FOREWORD

Parenting Adopted Teenagers by Rachel Staff is a valuable addition to our understanding of what is a complex, challenging, rewarding and, in many cases, emotionally exhausting experience.

The pioneering American psychologist and educator Granville Stanley Hall said in 1904 'Adolescence is a new birth'. Any parent of a teenager will recognize that! Teenagers didn't always exist but the cultural turmoil created by the Industrial Revolution caused us to invent a new generation and culturally we have been in a conflicted state of acceptance ever since, of the strangeness that can be the teenage child.

Rachel Staff talks about the features and challenges of 'normal' adolescence and reminds us of the factors that lie behind the behaviours and mood swings that any parent of a teenage child experiences. I observe first-hand the fascinating development of a child becoming a woman with my stepdaughter, some 15 to 20 years after my birth daughters went through their adolescence. It is at times amusing, frustrating, extraordinary and ultimately, for most parents, only occasionally a very rough transition to a steadier state of adulthood.

Rachel also reminds us that the pressures on teenagers now are greater than they have ever been. The pressures that social media, advertising, and easy access to pornography bring, sit on top of all the other more traditional risks and anxieties. Parenting teenagers well requires an understanding and empathy of what lies behind the stranger that has suddenly appeared in the home, combined with a high degree of resilience and humour. My poor late father, who never did anything wrong as a parent, must have been both hurt by and puzzled about why I didn't talk to him for a couple of years in my late teens. I just decided one day that I wasn't going to for no good reason.

For adoptive parents, the onset of teenage years poses a completely different set of feelings and challenges. The seminal research report *Beyond the Adoption Order* by Julie Selwyn and her team, referenced by Rachel, has exposed to a wider audience the extreme difficulties that too many adoptive parents experience as their children enter adolescence. Probably the most unhelpful thing that most adoptive parents hear at this stage of their parenting from well meaning friends and relatives is 'Ah, but most teenagers are like that.' They are not and Rachel combines in the early chapters of this book a summary of why teenagers are as they are and why adopted teenagers can be so different.

Most people reading this book will have enough of an understanding of the stages of child development and the effects of early childhood trauma and attachment issues to understand why the teenage years can be so very difficult for adopted children and their parents. But having understanding is one thing. Translating that into strategies for effective parenting of extreme behaviours is quite another, as is the need for professionals to understand that there is a different order of understanding and support required for these parents. Rachel helps us to understand the development and impact of a deep sense of shame that so many adopted teenagers share. Shame is also a word we at Adoption UK have heard a lot recently used by parents to describe themselves in talking about their experiences of child on parent violence. We also continue to hear too many examples of professionals not equipped with enough understanding of the issues that Rachel so clearly sets out.

This book is ambitious in what it sets out to cover. It addresses the issues I have highlighted above, it goes on to explore approaches and strategies for managing behaviour, adopted adolescents' mental health, the nature of relationships as they evolve with parents and peers and the first intimate partners. It also deals with the threatening issue, for many adoptive parents, of contact with birth parents. The powerful mix of teenage curiosity, high emotional intensity and feelings of loss, impulsiveness and risk taking are now facilitated by social media. Never has it been easier to find and get in touch with someone.

This book has a good balance of theory and practical assistance. Where it really stands out is in the significant use of case studies. Rachel draws on her years of highly relevant experience to provide numerous case studies. As Rachel points out, all children are different so not every case study will resonate with all adopters but there is enough here alongside the practical approaches and strategies to help most if not all adopters who experience difficulties with their teenage children.

One of the risks of exposing the extreme challenges some adoptive families experience as children go through adolescence is that it puts people off adopting. Rachel tackles this head on in her conclusion and her remarks resonate with everything I've ever heard from parents who have adopted. What those in challenging circumstances need is understanding, to feel they are not alone and practical advice and support. Rachel's book delivers this and I trust that it will become a well-thumbed reference for very many adopters.

Hugh Thornbery
Chief Executive, Adoption UK

Acknowledgements

I would like to thank all of the families and young people who have shared their experiences and stories with me. I would particularly like to thank the parents of the Parents of Adopted Teenagers Support Group in North London. Working with them has been a humbling and inspiring experience.

I would like to acknowledge my colleagues Jo Gordon and Val Forrest, co-facilitators of the parents' group; their skill and dedication has been very much appreciated. I would also like to acknowledge Peter Stevens, whose work for the North London Adoption and Fostering Consortium has enabled groups like the parents' group to exist and flourish. I would like to thank my colleagues at Adoptionplus who together make a fantastic team and, particularly, Ben and Elsie for their wise words in thinking about the book. Previous supportive and skilled colleagues, through whom I have learned so much, are too numerous to list, but my own 'adoption journey' has been particularly inspired by the Coventry Post-adoption Team (Gail, Sarah, Laura, Julia and Jane), previous colleagues at Family Futures and the many social workers I have worked with in the social work teams in North London.

I would like to say a special thank you to Cassie; it's been a pleasure to work with you, and your experiences and wise words about what it's like to be an adopted teenager will always stay with me!

Finally, I would like to thank my family and friends for their support. A particular thanks to Lily for her patience while my time has been taken up by writing and for generally being a pretty fabulous teenager all round!

About Adoptionplus

Adoptionplus is a voluntary adoption agency registered in 2008 to find families for older, harder-to-place children with complex needs.

It offers a new type of adoption service in the UK, one that recognizes how essential responsive, effective adoption support is. Adoptionplus decided to recruit a therapy team as part of its placement service, available to all its families whenever they need support. The therapy team is headed by a consultant clinical child psychologist and offers a range of trauma and attachment based therapies. It aims to ensure that the children it places for adoption not only have secure, loving and happy homes, but also that they truly have the opportunity to heal from their early trauma, learn how to have relationships, manage their feelings and live satisfying lives.

As part of its work, Adoptionplus was aware that children need a coherent sense of their past and an understanding of what has happened and why it may have happened. Many children believe that it is their fault that their birth parents couldn't look after them or abused and hurt them. They think that they are unlovable or bad and that they are responsible for all of the pain they have suffered. Adoptionplus believes that leaving children with these distorted self-beliefs will not only negatively impact the development of new, healthy attachment relationships with their adoptive or foster parents, but also is likely to lead to a life of ongoing emotional pain and not being able to gain the comfort and support of healthy emotional relationships with others, as it is difficult for children to believe that they are lovable. It becomes difficult to trust that other people genuinely care for them. Additionally, children may have a distorted view of their birth parents and may attribute positive qualities to them that they do not have. In turn these fantasies can be very unhelpful in the development of healthy attachment relationships with adoptive parents.

Adoptionplus sees contact as an opportunity to clarify the myths and promote a realistic and helpful understanding of past events. Seeing for themselves and understanding why their parents may have behaved as they did can correct children's distorted self-beliefs. Adoptionplus believes that this is enormously important to long-term emotional health.

As an agency, Adoptionplus also works with birth parents who have had their children removed and placed for adoption. These parents are often themselves confused about how they have ended up in the situation they are in, let alone knowing what to say to their children about it. In Adoptionplus's experience many parents would welcome support and guidance to help them help their children. With the right support, some parents are keen to apologize for mistakes they have made and clarify that none of it was their children's fault. In lots of ways Adoptionplus believes this can also be beneficial for the birth parents' emotional health. Their sense of self-worth can increase if they can feel that they are truly offering their child something that is helpful to them. Offering some feeling of resolution is better than the pain of none at all. This pain can often leave birth parents stuck in the trauma of losing their children and make it very difficult for them to move forward in their lives and can in fact lead to further deterioration of emotional health.

The more emotionally healthy birth parents are, the better it is for their children. In the current age of Facebook and the internet, there are clearly many benefits of investing in addressing unresolved issues as early as possible. Local authorities already spend resources on arranging and delivering contact services. Adoptionplus believes that this investment can be so much more beneficial if local authorities consider how they use contact time. Instead of it just being a space where resources are used to monitor and assess, it could be used to benefit significantly the emotional health of both the children and their birth parents. Adoptionplus is really interested in encouraging local authorities to review their understanding of their use of contact sessions and to consider how it could be so much more beneficial. In a time of limited resources, it seems sensible to look at improving something that local authorities are already doing and to consider how some changes could encourage numerous benefits.

Disclaimer

I have addressed this book directly to adopters, but I hope that others will read it and find it useful – social workers, foster carers and support workers who work with adopted teenagers and their families.

All of the stories I have included are a mix of lots of different stories and all the identities have been changed. The stories are accurate reflections of the reality of the adopted teenager's journey.

INTRODUCTION

Adoption today – who are the adopted teenagers we are discussing?

The teenage years, which span the ages between 12 and 25 (I am defining the period of adolescence as spanning these stages in line with contemporary understanding of the period of growth and maturation taking place in the brain during this developmental stage), can be a tumultuous time for many families. This key period of development presents many emotional challenges for young people and their families as the adolescent moves through a journey of individuation (individuation refers to the process of developing a unique sense of self) and separation and towards young adulthood. Teenagers must navigate a complex and challenging world. During this period they will face a range of challenges, some of which will be developmental. Important changes occur in the adolescent brain and in the physiological system as the biological drive prepares the young person for adulthood. Other challenges arise from the external demands of the education system and the expectations of adolescents as they prepare for further education or to become members of the job market. Today's teenagers also navigate a more complex, intrusive and challenging social world in which they need to be able to engage with social media and the wider 'online' world.

This book will explore the additional challenges that adolescence presents for today's adopted teenagers. The demographic of adopted teenagers I will be focusing on are those young people who were removed from their birth families in earlier childhood because of concerns about their birth family's capacity to keep them safe. They are the children who, for the main part, were judged to have suffered 'significant harm' within their birth parents' care. These young people will have experienced a range of traumatic experiences in their early years, which may have included: neglect, physical abuse, sexual abuse and emotional abuse. All of the young people will have experienced the loss of their birth families and (usually) subsequent carers as they moved through the care system before being placed for adoption. The intensity and extent of the young people's early life experiences will, of course, have varied but the majority of young adopted people in their teenage years in society today will have experienced adversity and loss in their early childhood. In exploring the experience of adopted young people and their parents I will therefore be focusing on the relationship between early loss and trauma and adolescence.

It is my experience, as a professional who has worked with adopted teenagers and their families for over 12 years, that this is a time of significant challenge for the family. Referrals requesting support from children's services and mental health services in the teenage years will include requests for support with: young people's emotional presentation and behaviours, mental health concerns, difficulties in family relationships, concerns in regard to the young person's identity, concerns about contact with birth family members, worries about peer relationships, early intimate relationships and education difficulties. Parents are usually requesting support for the young person but are also in great need of support for themselves.

In 2014, Selwyn, Wijedasa and Meakings published their research report *Beyond the Adoption Order: Challenges, Interventions and Adoption Disruption*.[1] This research, which explored adoption disruption and the challenges that adoptive families face, found that two thirds of adoption disruptions occurred during secondary school age. Some of the key factors highlighted by the research in regard to the teenage years are listed below.

- Many parents described a rapid escalation of challenging behaviour in their child as they approached puberty. Adopters reported that the children were on average 11 years old when difficulties began to escalate. Some saw the onset and escalation of difficulties at that time. For some this was a very sudden change in behaviour.[2]

- Difficulties included: oppositional behaviour, verbal aggression, physical aggression, destroying things, difficult behaviour in school, difficulty in forming friendships, sabotaging intended positive experiences, running away, actual or threatened self-harm, sexualized behaviour (age inappropriate), depression/low mood, anxiety/OCD, serious crime, making allegations against others, alcohol misuse and drug misuse.[3]

- In particular reference to aggression, much of it happened within the adoptive home and was violence intended to control and dominate. Parents found they had to change their own behaviour in response. Boys were more likely to use this violence. Children who had been aggressive from early on in the placement continued to be so as they got older. However, there was another group of children whose violence began around the time of puberty.[4]

* Many parents were physically injured as a result of the violence as the young person's physical strength grew, the balance of physical power shifting during this stage.[5]

This book will explore why these challenges occur, what parents can do to support their young people and themselves and what services need to provide for families during this time. I will be drawing on theory, to help us to understand adolescence itself, and also looking at how trauma and attachment can explain why this group of adolescents may travel a particularly rocky road in this developmental stage.

The influence of trauma, loss and attachment

Why do early experiences of loss and trauma still create difficulties in adolescence even though young people have had the benefit of secure and loving homes with adoptive parents?

An understanding of children's early attachment styles with birth parents, foster carers and then their adoptive parents are central considerations for professionals and parents when understanding the way in which adolescents will manage family, peer and early intimate relationships in the teenage years.

In Adoptionplus publication *Facilitating Meaningful Contact*, Price and Sydney[6] explain the theoretical perspective of attachment and trauma:

> John Bowlby's attachment theory postulates that babies have an innate behavioural system designed to elicit the care and protection of caregivers (usually mothers). Given the level of helplessness of babies, these behaviours help to ensure survival of the species. Mothers have a reciprocal system designed to help them bond with the baby and meet their needs. When babies and young children are feeling safe within their environment, their attachment behaviours are

complemented by exploratory behaviours, which are also instinctive. Therefore, the internal sense of security instilled (or downloaded) from the primary attachment relationship is transformed into a drive to explore the external world and all that comes with it.

Bowlby also developed the theory of the internal working model, which begins to emerge pre-verbally as the child forms general inferences about themselves and others based upon how they are treated by primary caretakers. As babies grow older their care-eliciting behaviours become more sophisticated and purposeful. The responses and behaviours of caregivers produce differing internal working models and attachment behaviours in children, which eventually organize into an attachment style. In the case of abuse and neglect, these inferences and the developing internal working model are likely to be negative, both in relation to the self and others. A child's perception of the world is prone to expecting threat, harsh responses or indifference.

The infant's internal working model develops within the context of a multisensory communication. This working model evolves within the developing right brain and is encoded in implicit unconscious memory. The sensitivity, tone and appropriateness of the parents'/caregivers' vocalizations, eye and body movements, sounds and smells all contribute to the development of the model and profoundly inform beliefs, which affect the child's ability to form loving relationships and healthy connections with others.

Attachment theory and methods of researching attachment security have played a significant role in illuminating our understanding of the psychological development of children and adults. Research into non-clinical populations has shown that 55 per cent of the adult population have 'secure' attachment status, therefore at least 45 per cent of us have an insecure style of relating. There are three insecure attachment presentations that have been identified as developing during early childhood. In non-clinical populations, the prevalence of insecure ambivalent resistant attachment is around 8 per cent, insecure avoidant 23 per cent and disorganized 15 per cent. Research into children brought up in neglectful or abusive environments shows that as many as 80 per cent develop disorganized attachments. These children behave unpredictably and have difficulty regulating their emotions. Disorganized attachment is strongly associated with later psychopathology.

Bowlby hypothesized that an infant's capacity to manage stress is developed within the relationship with the mother, with her responses shaping the infant's developing coping responses. The work of clinicians and neuroscientists such as Allan Schore are affirming Bowlby's theories and have deepened our understanding of the mechanisms and areas of the brain in the infant's developing capacity for affect regulation (which develops in the right hemisphere of the brain) and the central importance of the attachment relationship and role played by the mother or primary caregiver.

Research into the stress responses of toddlers who exhibited a disorganized attachment revealed that these children had higher cortisol levels and higher heart rates than all the other attachment classifications.

Neuroscience tells us that babies and toddlers' brains develop rapidly and sequentially, from the bottom (brain stem) to the top (cortex) and from the inside out. The neural systems which mediate social interaction, communication, empathy and the capacity to bond with others are all shaped by the nature, quantity and timing of early life relationships. Interpersonal experiences with primary caregivers literally shape the developing brain. The more a neural system is activated, the more that system changes to reflect the pattern of activation. Children exposed to significant threat will 're-set' their baseline state of arousal such that even when no external threats or demands are present they will be in a physiological state of persistent alarm. This means that when they do encounter even relatively small relationship stressors, the traumatized child will be more reactive and easily triggered into fight, flight or freeze responses. This increased baseline level of arousal and response to perceived threat plays a major role in the various behavioural and cognitive problems associated with the traumatized child.

Whilst young children may initially respond to fear by becoming hyperaroused, showing and acting out their distress through their behaviour, a second later-forming reaction to infant trauma is seen in dissociation, in which the child disengages from the stimuli in the external world. The child's dissociation in the midst of terror involves numbing, avoidance, compliance and restricted affect (the same pattern as adult PTSD [post-traumatic stress disorder]).

Van der Kolk *et al.* advocate moving away from labelling children with diagnoses such as reactive attachment or conduct disorders to using the term 'developmental trauma disorder'. This concept more accurately describes the consequences for babies and young children of living with the day-to-day exposure of multiple/chronic forms of developmentally adverse experiences, including neglect, physical/sexual abuse, witnessing domestic violence and abandonment.

The insights that attachment theory and neuroscience bring to our understanding of the needs of the developmentally traumatized and emotionally troubled child informs the work of some of our most eminent therapeutic clinicians and practitioners, such as Kim Golding and Dan Hughes.

If developmentally traumatized children are to be offered a realistic opportunity of developing an improved capacity for regulation and increased resilience, they first need to be placed within a low stress, safe and secure environment. Caregivers need to understand that new experience is 'filtered' through past experience, as the brain makes associations between sensory signals co-occurring in any given moment in time.

The child needs sensitively attuned carers who understand and meet the feelings that generate reactive behaviours. The child also needs a predictable, consistent, structured and nurturing routine, which is aimed at addressing their developmental stage (and needs) rather than chronological stage (and needs). Change occurs through consistent, nurturing, patterned, right-brained experiences, which require multiple repetitions as a means of supporting the development of new healthier neural connections. An image to describe this process is of layer upon layer of healthy interactions that eventually create a more solid foundation to a child's lived experience.

Children who are placed for adoption between the ages of 4 and 8 are considered 'older and hard-to-place'. A longitudinal study carried out by Kaniuk, Steele and Hodges into the changes in 'attachment representations' or 'internal working models' of children who were placed for adoption in this age group concluded that the previously maltreated children were able to develop internal working models of parental figures that were more responsive and caring. However, the previous internal working models of neglectful, abusive or rejecting parent figures continued to exist alongside, although with diminishing potency. During times of stress and change, however, the earlier working models are likely to be activated, evoking feelings of confusion and anxiety. On this point these researchers conclude, 'It is not possible to wipe out or remove memory traces of early negative experiences. Indeed, neurobiology indicates that traces of early negative experiences will remain indefinitely in the primitive structures of the brain.'[7]

Teenagers who are adopted have usually experienced the attuned, sensitive and nurturing care that they have needed following their early experiences of trauma and loss. The type of parenting that these young people have experienced will, of course, be varied in nature. Every family is unique and every parent will have brought their own strengths and vulnerabilities to their parenting role. No parenting experience is perfect and some adoptive parents will have been able to meet their child's particular emotional needs more than others. Sometimes this may be because parents have the advantage of parenting from a particularly secure base themselves; sometimes parents may have received effective support that has enabled them to adapt their parenting to the particular challenges that the impact of trauma and loss have presented for their children in earlier childhood. Regardless of the degree of strengths or vulnerabilities that parents bring to adoptive parenting, it is the case that the vast majority of parents set out with sincere and highly motivated intentions to provide a happy family life for themselves and the children they adopt. The adoptive parents I have worked with (whatever their vulnerabilities) have done the best they can in often very challenging circumstances.

The reality of neurobiology, which indicates that vulnerabilities can, and often do, remain in the brain, does however mean that despite the attuned and sensitive care that young people experience, the trauma of their early years will continue to impact on their development.

The initial tuning of the social-emotional brain circuitry and stress-response systems tends to keep running the same old programs even when presented with 'new' information in response to the old behaviours. Nature has ensured that we will not give up original strategies for survival so easily.[7]

These vulnerabilities often emerge or escalate in adolescent years because of the nature of the changes in the teenage brain during this stage and the particular challenges they face at this time of life.

The teenage brain

In his book, *Brainstorm*, Siegel[8] sets out the key changes that occur in the teenage brain:

> Brain changes during the early teen years set up four qualities of our minds during adolescence: novelty seeking, social engagement, increased emotional intensity, and creative exploration. There are changes in the fundamental circuits of the brain that make the adolescent period different from childhood. These changes affect how teens seek rewards in trying new things, connect with their peers in different ways, feel more intense emotions, and push back on the existing way of doing things to create new ways of being in the world. Each of these changes is necessary to create the important shifts that happen in our thinking, feeling, interacting and decision making during our adolescence.[9]

Each of the qualities of mind that are set up in adolescence prepare the young person in moving towards adulthood and potentially have both beneficial and negative effects for adolescents. Siegel identifies these 'upsides and downsides' below. I would add that for many adopted teenagers there are particular challenges within each of the areas, which can mean that they are more likely to experience the 'downsides' of these qualities. These are outlined at this point but will be explored more fully throughout the themes within the book.

'Novelty seeking'[10] is crucial in adolescence; the young person needs to prepare to begin to 'step out into the world' and the increased drive for rewards in the brain encourages the adolescent to try new things. This creates a new passion for life and adventure. The downsides of this are that risk taking can result in dangerous behaviours and impulsivity without reflection can increase risk. Adopted adolescents can struggle with dangerous risk taking because of vulnerabilities present as a result of their earlier development and in relation to the additional emotional challenges they may face in areas such as identity development and attachment relationships.

'Social engagement'[11] provides a new quality of friendships that can provide essential emotional support as young people begin the process of separation from their families. The downsides of this can emerge for young people if they are isolated from adults and surrounded by other teens, as risk taking can increase. For many adopted young people this area may pose particular challenges because they may struggle to maintain their capacity to use their attachment relationships with their parents in adolescence and 'direct themselves out' prematurely to rely almost exclusively on peer networks. Adopted teenagers may also struggle to form and maintain peer relationships, which could mean that they lack the essential support network that these relationships can provide.

'Increased emotional intensity'[12] can help to increase engagement in life and in new relationships. The downside of this is that intense emotion can be overwhelming. Many adopted adolescents are likely to struggle with emotional regulation as a result of their early experiences and will often have to cope with potentially overwhelming emotions of loss, anger and rejection resulting from their early experiences.

'Creative exploration'[13] – the adolescent's new conceptual thinking and abstract reasoning – allows questioning of the status quo. As teenagers increasingly engage with the world around them and prepare to become fully participating members of society, they are often engaged in an exciting process of questioning and analysing of the world around them and who they are in relation to it. The downside of this can be that searching for the meaning of life can lead to a crisis of identity, vulnerability to peer pressure and a lack of direction and purpose. For adopted young people, the formation of a positive identity is particularly challenging.

In summary, the vulnerabilities that adopted adolescents already bring to the teenage years, the root of which are in their early experiences of trauma and loss, can result in a 'double whammy' of challenge in all of these key areas. In addition, adolescent years are times of change (hormonal and physical changes are, of course, a significant impact on young people during this time) and stress, conditions within which insecure attachment patterns can re-emerge. Another important neurological process that can impact on the adolescent's vulnerability during this time is that of pruning.

> Pruning occurs in the teenage brain because of the need for the brain to 'remodel' itself. It is letting go of connections in the brain that aren't needed as it refines what it needs for adult life. Pruning is a necessary process but it can expose vulnerabilities for adopted teenagers because of their early developmental trauma effectively 'unmasking deficiencies'.[14]

Pruning, along with hormonal changes and alterations in how genes are expressed, shapes our neural activity and synaptic growth and makes the brain's functioning change dramatically during the teenage years.[15]

Heightened stress can also accelerate the pruning process, leaving the brain more vulnerable. What remains of the number of neurons and their connections can be insufficient to balance mood or thought for vulnerable young people. Many adopted young people will be experiencing heightened levels of stress as they progress through adolescence because of their additional vulnerabilities.[16]

The adopted teenager then, faces particular challenges in adolescence resulting from the vulnerabilities created by their early experiences of trauma and loss, the neurological changes that occur in adolescence and the physiological changes that occur during this period. He or she experiences these profound changes and vulnerabilities within the context of the external pressures of their social world and educational demands.

For some adolescents, the impact of these challenges can be overwhelming and highly confusing. Young people who may have seemed to manage reasonably well before this stage may find that their previous adaptive strategies are no longer enough in managing in key areas of their life.

That said, childhood defences against too much emotional pain often fail to hold in the teenage years. This is due to all the hormonal, body, brain and psychological changes. This means that early childhood experiences of terror, abandonment, shame or loss, successfully defended against in childhood, can be triggered in the teenage years, resulting in intense emotional outbursts and turmoil. This can happen without the teenager having any idea about the connection between what they are feeling now and what has happened to them in the past.[17]

Understanding the relationship between the past and the present when providing support

Adoptive parents may question whether they have provided 'good enough' parenting for their teenager in earlier childhood if they are experiencing difficulties in adolescence. Parents may have experienced improvements for their child in earlier and mid childhood and may feel alarmed that the 'ground gained' in emotional and psychological terms has been lost as their teenager starts to experience difficulties they haven't seen before or to revert to previous difficulties. The confusion that adoptive parents experience as they witness their child struggling during teenage years in a way they hadn't anticipated can also be mirrored by professionals and services.

Services may assume that the difficulties they are assessing in adoptive families are a result of poor parenting by the adoptive parents (after all, shouldn't the child be in better shape by now, they've been with the parents for ages!). Services often have a lack of understanding of the complexity of the relationship between past and present development and adolescence itself. However, interpreting difficulties in current functioning as being entirely attributable to the adoptive parent's parenting can result in inaccurate assessment and, at worst, punitive approaches to addressing difficulties.

Dan Siegel comments upon the differences for adolescents with insecure and secure attachment difficulties as follows:

> With a history of insecure attachment, our brains may not enter the adolescent period with the same baseline integrative growth that a securely attached person has been able to develop in childhood.[18]

In contrast:

> The benefits of secure early experiences mean that we enter adolescence with more integrated prefrontal functions which help to: regulate the body, attune to the self and others, balance our emotions, maintain flexibility, soothe our fears, have insight into and empathy for ourselves and others with a good grounding in a sense of morality.[19]

Many adopted teenagers will not have had the opportunity to develop these qualities fully prior to adolescence. The adolescent brain, firing on all cylinders from the amygdala (the emotional brain) is also characterized by immature and poorly developed prefrontal functioning. They are without the benefit of this 'top-down' moderating influence on their emotional responses; they are therefore experiencing a double whammy, which is likely to make their emotional experience during this stage even more 'wobbly'.

Adoptive families will of course have their own difficulties – things do go wrong, adoptive parents have often been living with very challenging situations for a long time and these difficulties can impact on their parenting. In this book I will discuss the need for effective services to be able to balance needs arising from the impact of early experiences and the impact of these on adopted teenagers and their families in the present in order to support young people and their families effectively.

Although much of this book focuses on the difficulties that arise for this demographic of adopted adolescents, it does so with a message of hope that with sufficient support this challenging stage of development also presents an opportunity for hope and change. The very fact that the changing nature of the teenage brain throws up challenges and exposes vulnerabilities means that this is an opportunity for those vulnerabilities to be met. The brain's plasticity, particularly at this stage of development, means that it can be influenced in a positive way. There is the possibility for positive change within relationships and indeed it is the parent–child relationship that still offers the best chance for this during this sometimes-tumultuous time of change.

Themes discussed

The chapters in this book explore some of the key areas that can pose particular challenges for adoptive families during adolescence. The chapters give focus to the areas of: the emotional experience of the teenage years, mental health considerations, changing relationships within the family, emerging identity issues, contact considerations, peer relationships and early intimate relationships. There is also a focus on the importance of support for young people and parents respectively during the adolescent period. The combined influence of the developmental tasks of the teenage years as well as the impact of the teenager's early life experiences will be explored throughout the chapters.

There are important elements of adoption and adolescence that I am not able to address within the book; unfortunately there isn't sufficient space to do so. In many areas I will be touching on topics that parents may wish to explore further and in more depth. References to useful resources will be provided, which I hope will be helpful. I am also particularly mindful that I am not addressing particular considerations that are present for many adoptive families. These include: transracial and transcultural considerations, adoptions within family and friends networks, same-sex couple (and single-parent) adoptions and inter-country adoptions. I have not addressed the issue of education, which I am aware is also a very important issue for many adoptive families (however, reference is made to the excellent work covered in Louise Bomber's (2011) book *What About Me?*,[20] which addresses the particular challenges within education). My intention is to retain the focus of this book on the impact of young people's experiences on their relationships and developing sense of self. Many of these will have universal elements that are applicable to adopted young people, whatever the context of their particular adoptive families.

Representing the parents' and adolescents' views

Each chapter contains aspects of the experiences of the adoptive parents I have worked with over the years. Their experiences, observations and understandings of the particularly unique journey they travel with their traumatized teenagers are important. In conveying their experiences I hope to provide a message to other adoptive parents that they are not alone and that there are many challenges but also hopeful messages in relation to support and strategies for this period in family life.

Observations from some of the adopted teenagers I have worked with are also included in the chapters. Like their parents, I am often humbled by their persistence, bravery and resilience in the face of the challenges they encounter.

Chapter One

KEY EMOTIONAL THEMES FOR ADOPTED TEENAGERS

This chapter will explore some of the key emotional challenges that can be present for adopted adolescents and their parents during this period of development. The focus in this chapter is on those emotional states and the resulting behaviours that, in my experience, adoptive parents frequently seek support in addressing. The following chapter will look to specific behaviours that adopters raise as being of concern with an ongoing focus on the developmental and emotional difficulties that may lie beneath them.

The impact of emotions in the brain of adopted teenagers

Contemporary culture is rich in reference to the emotional struggles of adolescence. Moody, angst ridden, angry, aggressive, excitable, intense and depressive are just some of the emotional states that will be identified by adults if asked to think about the emotional experience of adolescence. The emotional life of adolescents can be full of excitement with intense, joyous times but it can also be extremely challenging. Indeed, it is often the more challenging aspects of the adolescent's emotional life that are brought to mind by those reflecting on this time of development. This is perhaps partly because the emotional intensity of teenage years can pose particular challenges for those adults involved in the care of teenagers as well as wider society in general. Popular perceptions of adolescents' emotional states are often that they are 'out of control'. This message is also reinforced by a media narrative that focuses our attention on the aggressive, impulsive and despairing aspects of the adolescent emotional states with their resulting behaviours and impact on society. I am often reminded of the sense of threat that adults and wider society perceive as emanating from the adolescent's emotional presentation when reading stories in the news (which are usually focused on the more dramatic and destructive outcomes of adolescent's emotional struggles). It can be perceived as uncontainable, frightening and destructive, but how well informed are these commonly held beliefs?

In the introduction I briefly outlined the way in which changes in the teenager's neurological development (as well as hormonal changes) can impact on the young person and how early experiences of trauma and loss may combine to increase vulnerabilities for young people. How may the teenagers and their parents feel the impact of these factors in family life when we are thinking about key emotional themes that arise for adopted adolescents?

Parents of adolescents will often comment that their teenagers are just 'so emotional' and indeed they are. For those living with teenagers, it can feel as though one is living with unpredictable and frequent swings between different emotional states that can seem out of proportion to the events or triggers that preceded them. Sometimes it simply isn't possible to identify whatever triggered the adolescent into a big emotional response. For parents, the emotional life of the teenager can often feel perplexing and exhausting. For adoptive parents though, their experience of their teenager's emotional lives is often that it is 'the usual teenage stuff' with bells on! Parents of adopted teenagers often describe the unpredictability, extreme nature and frequency of emotional mood swings as leaving them feeling as though they are walking on eggshells.

Influences on the brain's emotions during adolescence

In the introduction I highlighted Daniel Siegel's description of one of the qualities of mind that that are set up in adolescence as being that of increased emotional intensity.[1] The teenage brain takes on a new emotional intensity so that the adolescent is able to increase his or her engagement in life and in new relationships. This is important and serves a crucial developmental function. The intense experiencing of emotion can be a wonderful thing in teenage years, when those experiences are pleasurable ones of joy, connection, excitement, welcoming of new experiences and indeed experiencing the world anew. The challenges, of course, arise when the emotions experienced are less positive, as these too are experienced with an intensity that can feel overwhelming for both the young person and their parents.

Put simply, in neurological terms, the emotional lower brain in teenage years is activated more readily than it is when we are children or in adulthood. As teenagers we have a more immediate emotional response that is not filtered by cortical reasoning. Our prefrontal cortex, which is necessary for balancing emotions/having insight and empathy, is not fully developed during this period of development. As a consequence our emotional responses are taking place without the benefit of our 'cognitive brain' monitoring and managing our subcortical world.[2]

Adopted teenagers are often entering this stage of development while carrying the impact of their early experiences of loss and trauma and the consequences of these experiences on their earlier brain development. They are often entering this heightened period of emotional vulnerability with less well-integrated prefrontal functions and therefore a compromised ability to regulate and balance emotions.

It is, then, particularly unfortunate that the particular emotional challenges adopted teenagers will need to face are often far more challenging and intense than those of their peers who are not adoptees. The following emotional themes are some of those that prove most challenging for young people and their parents who seek support.

Loss and the particular considerations for the adopted teenager's brain

Creative exploration is another quality of mind set up in the teenage brain at this developmental stage. Conceptual thinking and abstract reasoning enable teenagers to question who they are in relation to the world. These changes also bring a new ability for adolescents to both comprehend and understand loss and particularly the experience of loss within their own lives. Loss is one of the many 'meaning-of-life' themes that teenagers will explore and sometimes struggle with at this developmental stage. Managing and processing feelings of loss in the adolescent years is a natural part of this stage of development. Adolescence marks the 'beginning of the end' of childhood; young people are in the process of separating from their families and individuating. This stage of development is a transition between earlier childhood and early adulthood; the passing of time and the changes that young people are managing will inevitably give rise to feelings of loss. For adopted teenagers though, this theme can be a particularly painful and challenging one, as they are a group of young people who have experienced more loss than the majority of their peers. The full extent of earlier losses is fully comprehended for the first time at this stage.

The teenage brain provides a new capacity for abstract thought and the processing of loss. This means that adopted young people will begin to experience the full meaning of their early losses in life in a new and intense way as they move through adolescence.[3]

As well as being removed from their birth family, many adopted young people will have also separated from one or more sets of foster carers (many children will have stayed with these carers for at least two years). Young people may well also have experienced the loss of siblings, friendships and many other elements of their younger lives (such as schools) that were significant to them.

Many adopted teenagers are also grappling with the impending 'loss' of their childhood within their adoptive family at this developmental stage. Some will experience this as a premature loss and express their feelings that they have not had enough of their childhood within their adoptive families, compounding the feeling that many adolescents hold that they are not yet ready for being 'grown up' and being separate from their parents. This is experienced in parallel with feeling the losses of their first families for many young adopted teenagers.

• • • • • • • • • CHARLOTTE AGED 17 • • • • • • • • • •

Charlotte had had direct contact with her birth family throughout her teenage years. Her adoptive parents had been sensitive to her needs in relation to the contact and had supported her so that this could happen safely and with their support (this will be discussed further in Chapter Eight). Managing relationships and attachments to both her birth and adoptive families had not been easy for Charlotte, but she did have an attachment to both of her families. Charlotte worried about loss, particularly as she approached her

18th birthday. She worried that her parents would retire and go travelling: 'I don't feel old enough to be on my own.' She worried that her parents would become ill. She also, though, thought about the fact that she would have to endure the loss of two sets of parents when they died: 'I'm going to have to do it twice you know.' Alongside these preoccupations of loss was also an awareness of other losses she felt (at times) quite keenly: the loss of time within her adoptive family: 'I haven't had enough yet'; and loss of the time she could have spent with birth family members, in particular her birth sister, to whom she was close.

. . . .

The extent of and degree to which this loss is felt will of course vary widely between individuals, but for many young people, loss will be experienced in a more profound and keenly felt way during this period. For some young people, the experience of loss at this time may feel overwhelming and move them into a profound state of helplessness and despair.

. . . . JESSICA AGED 15 . . . .

Jessica's maternal grandmother had died soon after her 15th birthday. Jessica had become increasingly withdrawn from family life. Her parents were extremely concerned that she appeared low in mood and was becoming increasingly isolated. She was rejecting of her parents' attempts to engage her and spent most of her time alone in her bedroom. Her behaviour was a contrast to her previous presentation, which her parents described as 'typically adolescent'. Although Jessica had always spent time alone, she had also spent time with her family and had not previously been as withdrawn. Jessica had been referred for social-work support.

After spending some time getting to know Jessica I broached the subject of her grandmother's death. I noted that her parents felt that she had become more withdrawn after this and asked Jessica if she thought that had happened. Jessica agreed that she had and as we explored what she thought was going on for her, the extent to which this loss had triggered much wider fears of loss became clear. Jessica's grandmother's death and the grieving that followed had brought to the fore Jessica's new awareness of her earlier life losses. This had triggered some very profound fears for her and a very real sense of 'wobbliness' and fragility in her realization that there were many more losses that she would need to face over her lifetime. For the first time she began to process the reality of the losses of her birth parents (from whom she had been removed at the age of two years), the siblings who had been placed for adoption (and with whom she had had no contact since) and the foster carers she had stayed with for three years. Jessica felt overwhelmed with grief and her awareness and fear of the future losses she would face. As she observed, she had already lost her birth family when she was removed from them, and she knew that one day her adoptive parents would die and also that her birth parents would die and she would need to revisit this loss again. For Jessica, this was just too much. She had begun to withdraw emotionally from her parents; this made some kind of sense to Jessica: if she wasn't as close to them emotionally she wouldn't have to face further pain as a result of the losses she knew must come. Jessica's understanding was that she was protecting herself; what was really happening of course was that her loss was so much harder to bear because she was unable to use her parents for the emotional support and nurture she so desperately needed. Jessica needed time to be able to reflect on her earlier life losses and give name to the feelings she was experiencing that had been triggered by the loss of her grandmother. She agreed that we could share these thoughts together with her parents, which helped them to make sense of her responses and empathize with how hard it must be for her. In doing so, Jessica was gradually able to reduce her anxieties and to feel less fearful about relying on her parents for love and support.

Brodinsky, Schechter and Marantz Henig[4] also highlight this period of change and developmental as a time when grief will re-emerge and express itself in a variety of ways: 'Grieving almost always follows loss. It has many emotional and behavioral manifestations: shock, anger, depression, despair, helpless-ness, and hopelessness.'

While Jessica's response to loss was one of despair, withdrawal and helplessness, other young people may experience heightened levels of anger as a part of the grieving process. This may particularly be the case when a young person's sense of loss is combined with painful feelings of rejection.

• • • • • • • • • • KIERAN AGED 14 • • • • • • • • • •

Kieran had been placed for adoption at an early age (before he was 18 months old). His birth mother had been involved with a violent partner and had not been able to end the relationship despite being advised by social services that if she didn't do so, the risk to Kieran was so great that he would removed from her care. Kieran's adoptive parents had always been open with him in regard to his early history and had tried to place his birth mother's inability to leave her partner within the context of her vulnerabilities and dependence upon him. Kieran though, felt a profound sense of loss, rejection and rage at his birth mother's abandonment of him. He directed a great deal of his anger towards his adoptive mother and his parents were concerned about his relationship with female teachers and some of his peers. Kieran was hypersensitive to any perceived injustice that he felt was directed either towards him or others and was often in trouble at school for 'taking up the cause' of friends or peers who he felt had been wronged. Kieran's parents needed support to understand that the cognitive explanation they were providing for him was not enough in itself to help Kieran process and make sense of his feelings about his early history. With his parents' support, Kieran was given the time and focus to work through his early life history. His feelings of abandonment and loss were met with acceptance and empathy, and exploration was given to how these feelings were impacting on his life. This was important. Kieran's parents were anxious to ease his distress by providing logical explanations to try and explain his birth mother's decisions. Kieran did indeed need these explanations in order to make sense of these early events, but first he needed to have the experience of having his emotions met and 'felt' by his parents and the therapist. He needed to feel their empathy. Importantly, his feelings about his birth mother were validated as being entirely understandable. His pain in response to his experience of loss, abandonment and rejection was still very much present whatever the reasons that lay behind those early life events and indeed was being experienced with a new intensity by his adolescent brain. He was given a strong message of acceptance and empathy for those very powerful feelings and support in naming his feelings of grief and anger as being located in his feelings towards his birth mother. His parents were supported to talk about how they would have protected him from those early experiences if they had been able to and his mother in particular spoke about her commitment to Kieran, her certainty that she would never reject or abandon him and her understanding that it must be difficult for him to trust that this wouldn't happen because of his birth mother's actions. At a later stage in the work Kieran was provided with a more detailed and fuller explanation of his birth mother's own life experiences so that he could develop a deeper understanding of why she was unable to make the right decisions or choices. Kieran's ability to 'place' his feelings of pain and grief where they belonged helped him to increase his trust in his adoptive mother and understand his anger towards her, which helped to begin to improve their relationship (and his relationships towards other women in his life).

Loss and grief do, of course, emerge in different ways for young people and will be experienced in differing intensities (a particularly useful reference in understanding the nature of loss for the adopted person is *The Primal Wound* by Nancy Verrier[5]) and often combine with other painful feelings. Parents are often unaware that behaviours are indications that the young person is struggling with loss and grief, and young people are often unaware of this themselves. Chapter Three will discuss useful approaches and strategies in responding to this theme, but to be aware that it is likely to be a common struggle for many adopted teenagers is a useful starting point in being alert to what may underlie confusing and distressing behaviours.

Conflict and anger: what are the particular considerations for adopted teenagers?

While grief may contribute to increased levels of anger for some adopted teenagers, it is the case that adolescence is a time in which we see increased levels of conflict and an increased intensity in emotions, including anger, anyway. Increased levels of anger during this developmental stage occur partly because of a range of physiological changes in the adolescent. Hormonal and chemical changes can lead to increased aggression: higher testosterone levels in boys and higher oestrogen levels in girls have been found to increase levels of aggression in teenagers for example.[6]

The frustrations of the teenage years in the inevitable struggle for more autonomy may lead to increased levels of conflict and anger. As teenagers push for more control and against their parents' value systems, conflict inevitably arises and may result in angry outbursts. Questioning parents' values, pushing against boundaries and challenging household rules are very much a natural part of the teenage experience. Adolescents need to do this as part of the separation and individuation process. The qualities of mind of emotional intensity and creative exploration combine in increasing the intensity of emotional responses and the need to question the status quo and push against boundaries. Parent–child conflict in the adolescent years is developmentally appropriate and experienced by the vast majority of (if not all!) families during this developmental stage. In *Nurturing Natures*, Music describes this as occurring across many species: 'Adolescents need to move away from parental control and take risks. In many species one sees increased interaction with peers, risk taking and more fighting with parents.' [7]

Teenagers then, are already prone to move into higher levels of conflict and may experience more intense feelings of anger because of the need to push against the status quo and hormonal changes, and their emotional responses are likely to be firing with intensity from the amygdala without the benefit of 'top-down' brain monitoring. Additionally, the way in which teenagers' brains read facial signals and non-verbal communications generally, can contribute towards a move into the 'fight' response.

> When adults see strong facial signals such as fear, scans show that their pre frontal cortex normally fires. With adolescents it is usually the amygdala, that more primitive region to do with flight or fight responses. [8]

The additional challenges for many adopted teenagers in managing anger are often related to the vulnerabilities they carry in being able to emotionally regulate effectively. They will have a much higher 'baseline arousal' to minor stresses because of their early experiences within stressful environments. Their stress response systems have become hypersensitive; for teenagers with brains that are highly sensitive to moving to the fight-or-flight responses, those responses can also be very rapid – the amygdala is even more reactive.

Adolescents who are sensitive to perceived threat are more likely to 'read' facial signals and other social cues as signalling potential danger when, actually, those signals may be communicating very different emotional states. The impact of this sensitivity to, and misreading of, others' emotional states can result in low-level conflict easily escalating to much more extreme responses. This does, of course, occur within the adolescent's social world but is also an often frustrating (and sometimes frightening) feature of conflict within the young person's family relationships.

• • • • • • • • • • MICHAEL AGED 17 • • • • • • • • • •

Michael had been out with friends for most of the weekend. He had returned home in the early hours of Sunday morning. Michael's father didn't mind that Michael had been out with friends – he wanted him to be going out and having fun – but Michael was not good at checking in with his parents to let them know he was OK. He hadn't replied to his mother's texts and she had been particularly worried about him. Michael's father was worried about his wife and the strain she was under and he resolved to speak to Michael about the need to check in with them when he was out for extended periods of time. On approaching Michael the next day, he was tired and feeling quite frazzled. He approached the subject by asking Michael if he'd had a good weekend; Michael was immediately 'on alert' and his body tensed ready for what he anticipated to be an impending fight with his father. His father said that he was glad he was getting out and having fun but that it was really important that he replied to texts or calls when his parents tried to contact him. Michael's response was defensive: 'I knew you were going to have a go at me, I could see it on your face as soon as you came in, I don't know why you have to make such a big deal out of everything.'

Michael's father's irritation was starting to rise. 'Look, I'm just saying that you need to show your mother the courtesy of replying to her messages – she worries.'

'Oh god, here we go, here comes the lecture. I can't do anything without you having a go at me – why are you so angry, it's not like I'm a kid anymore?'

Michael's father was starting to get annoyed. 'Look, I'm just saying that you need to show some consideration – we don't ask much of you, I don't know why you always have to have this attitude.'

'What are you talking about? It's not my attitude, you came in pissed off, shouting at me – you've totally ruined my weekend now.'

• •

The impact of these interactions can be both frustrating and perplexing for parents. The reactive nature of Michael's response also left no room for any resolution of what was a fairly low-level situation. Anger blocks the capacity for our higher-cortical, reasoned and balanced responses to make sense of and respond to situations in a more balanced and effective way.

Teenagers I have worked with have also expressed the fact that sometimes anger just 'feels good'; it can help them to feel strong and almost invincible in the powerful impact it can have on others. The reality is that it can feel a lot more comfortable and empowering than the much more vulnerable feelings that it masks. Many adopted young people are desperately trying to manage huge feelings of sadness and vulnerability. Hiding these behind a shield of anger can feel protective and empowering: 'The anger is a better "friend" than sadness in some ways.'[9]

However, high levels of anger and aggression also feel frightening to young people. The feelings of power that teenagers may experience in their anger are often accompanied by high levels of fear about the lack of control they have over it.

• • • • • • • • • • JORDAN AGED 16 • • • • • • • • • • •

Jordan's parents were extremely worried about the level of anger he was displaying at home. He had frequent angry outbursts, which often led to physical aggression. He would kick doors, had pushed his father over and had punched his mother on the arm. Jordan told his parents that he liked being angry – it made him feel good, and he didn't care that he hurt others when he was angry. During his therapeutic work Jordan completed a sand tray in which he was asked to show the relationships in his family. Jordan chose a knight figure to represent himself but also a dragon, which he placed alongside it. He identified his choice of these figures as representing different aspects of his anger. The knight was strong and could defend himself but the dragon would sometimes take over and when this happened he became frightened that the fire would destroy the other figures in the sand tray (representing his parents and other family members). Jordan then placed a red flag in front of his figures; he explained that he wished there was a flag or a red traffic light that could alert the knight when the dragon was going to step forward. Jordan's anger did indeed feel like a powerful and defensive force when conflict escalated, but he was frightened when this began to feel out of control and had the potential to destroy his relationships. Jordan was clear that he wanted some help in finding his own 'red flag' while not losing the capacity to feel strong in his defence of himself.

It is important to state that for many adopted teenagers anger is a valid emotional response to the reality of the experiences they have endured. Young people may well have had a loving and happy life within their adoptive families; however this does not necessarily take away the profoundly unjust and painful experiences of their early years. The adolescent brain provides a new capacity for young people to understand the reality of their early experiences and to have an emotional response to these experiences that is new in its intensity. There is, though, a difference between anger and 'rage'. Rage is an unregulated, overwhelming emotional state (Jordan's dragon).

> Rage is a massive disorganization of the self... In an outburst of rage, there have been such high levels of tension in the child's body and mind that he experiences a desperate,

uncontrollable need to discharge it, whether physically or verbally.[10]

Shame and the particular considerations for adopted teenagers

Shame is an emotional state that is less likely to be as familiar to us as other states such as happiness, sadness, anger, despair and so on. It is, though, an important feeling to be aware of, as it may often be present in teenagers' experiences generally and is particularly present for many adopted teenagers.

Shame is an overwhelming feeling that is often experienced by young people who have suffered from early trauma and lack of attuned caregiving. In *Nurturing Attachments*, Golding describes shame as follows:

> Shame is an affect, a complex emotion that develops later than the development of more straightforward feelings such as anger, joy or sadness. Shame is uncomfortable for children and therefore children will learn to limit shame-inducing behaviors. In this sense it is protective, because it helps children to behave in a way that is safe and helps them to develop relationships.[11]

The roots of shame can be found in early development. In toddler years, parents will often need to give children warnings or tell them 'no' in order to keep the child safe or behave in a socially acceptable way. All parents will be familiar with this testing stage of early development within which they can often feel that they are constantly 'telling their child off'. Shame begins to develop in these early years because when children are reprimanded they experience a 'break' in the relationship with their parent. The child briefly experiences his or her parent's displeasure with his or her actions (whether this is because they have tried to run into the road, touch a hot oven, eat something off the floor – the toddler years are made up of many such instances!). This is an unpleasant feeling: 'My mum/ dad is cross with me/I am cross with them/I don't feel close to them.' Parents will, however, usually follow this 'break' in the relationship in having to reprimand their child with reassurance and comfort. They will explain why they had to reprimand the child and ensure that the child understands that it was his or her behaviour that was being addressed. The parent 're-attunes' to the child's emotional state and makes sense of the experience after it happened. In time the child develops an experience of guilt rather than shame, understanding that it was the behaviour that was wrong rather than they themselves. Guilt, in contrast to shame, is a useful emotion when experienced in the right proportion. It helps us to develop a conscience and empathy.

Parents who struggle to understand and meet their child's emotional needs often, don't manage to do this well. Young children only receive the experience of the adult's anger, the telling off, the 'rupture' in the relationship without any re-attunement, comfort or 'making sense of' what has happened. In these circumstances children are left with an unregulated sense of shame that is overwhelming. Their experience is that they themselves are 'bad'. They will often re-experience this feeling over and over again.

Additionally, many young children will experience abuse over which they have no control or ability to make any sense of beyond their understanding that they must somehow have caused it. Intense feelings of humiliation and powerlessness compound the child's experience of shame. The child feels shameful, never quite good enough to belong: 'Traumatic and frightening experiences that cause the victim to feel powerless and helpless are usually accompanied by intense feelings of shame and humiliation.'[12]

Many adopted teenagers will have endured repeated experiences of shame in their early childhood. This toxic emotion is a frightening and unbearable one. It may well have persisted throughout the young person's childhood or emerged with a new intensity as the young person moved into the boundary-testing adolescent years (which has many parallels to the boundary-testing toddler years when the shame first developed). It is not unusual for adopted teenagers to move into shame and be overwhelmed by it.

> Shame in traumatized teenagers is a feeling of one's very 'self' being utterly flawed, defective and worthless. Teenagers who have been severely traumatized often feel a sense of shame, as they truly believe (either consciously or subconsciously) through their experiences that they are bad and unlovable.[13]

In *You Think I'm Evil*, Taransaud highlights the adolescent's new awareness of others' perceptions of him or her as also potentially heightening the sense of shame experienced.[14] Shame can be a particularly vulnerable state for adolescents, who are so newly and acutely aware of the way others perceive them and the meaning of whom they are. The adolescents who experiences high levels of shame will often use one or more options of defending themselves against this deeply uncomfortable feeling. One of these defences may be anger.

• • • • • • • • • KATHERINE AGED 13 • • • • • • • • •

Katherine was messing around with her friends at school, one of her friends told a joke and Katherine clearly didn't understand it, joining in with her version of a punchline that completely 'missed the mark'. Her friend laughed and teased: 'That's not what I was on about you idiot!' Katherine felt a surge of shame – her internal voice told her that yes indeed she was an idiot, too stupid to be a part of friends having a laugh, everyone must be laughing at her, she could never get anything right and they probably all said that about her all the time. Completely dysregulated she turned on her friend: 'Don't call me stupid you bitch,' and pushed her into the wall.

* *

> The painful feelings of inadequacy and self disgust that shame invokes blocks effective self-reflection and prevents the 'thinking brain' from moderating aggressive impulses.[15]

Whilst shame may present itself in rage it can also be present in: denial (lying), deflecting blame or minimizing incidents. Some examples of these experiences and responses may occur in situations such as those below.

* * * * * * * * * * * JODY AGED 15 * * * * * * * * * * * *

Jody was told off for lying about saying that she was going to the cinema when she actually went to a party. Her father told her that he didn't appreciate her lying and that she would be grounded for the next two weeks. Jody reacted with fury: 'You don't trust me, I can't believe you checked up on me, it's your fault for never letting me go out, I didn't even really lie because I told you I was with friends. I didn't actually say that I was going to the cinema you just assumed that, it was no big deal, you never think anything good of me, if you trusted me I wouldn't have to lie, you've always blamed me for everything that goes wrong, I wish you'd never adopted me, you've always hated me, I've never been good enough for you…'

* *

* * * * * * * * * * SIMON AGED 15 * * * * * * * * * * *

Simon had been to a parents' evening at his school. The reports had generally been positive; he was doing OK but underachieving in his grades because he was often distracted. The teachers' messages to his parents were that he had lots of potential but needed to focus more. On the way home in the car Simon was very quiet, his parents reflected that they were pleased with is progress but asked him how he thought he could improve on his concentration. Simon replied with intensity that it was impossible to concentrate in any of the classes, none of the teachers could keep control of the pupils, all of the kids had the same problem, it wasn't a good enough school, his friends were much worse than he was, it was them who distracted him, if the school wasn't 'so crap' he would be fine…

Parents can find these responses very confusing and it is often difficult to both recognize shame itself and identify the triggers into shame. It is, though, crucial to be aware of the presence of shame if we are to understand and support young people who are so impacted by it.

Low mood, anxiety and isolation: why is the teenage brain particularly vulnerable?

Many adolescents will struggle with low mood and anxiety at some point during this stage of development. As I have already discussed, this is a time of significant change and new awareness. 'Teenage angst' has long been a well-used phrase within popular culture and for good reason. For adopted adolescents though, the additional challenges they face mean that they are particularly vulnerable to anxiety and low mood to a degree that can impede their ability to participate in and enjoy life. This can sometimes lead to young people becoming withdrawn and isolated (as we saw with Jessica on page 40). Adopted adolescents who struggle with shame and low self-esteem will often struggle to engage with the social world. Young people with low self-esteem (emanating from feelings of rejection, self-blame for their earlier experiences and awareness of difference to their peers, for example) may not have any anticipation that they can succeed with activities or relationships – how could they when they are so worthless? This can create a profound feeling of helplessness. These young people may also have poor self-care skills, paying less attention than their peers to their appearance and general hygiene. Their bedrooms will often reflect their low self-esteem and be neglected and chaotic. These emotional states can be experienced by parents as laziness and lack of motivation on the young person's part.

• • • • • • • • • • RYAN AGED 16 • • • • • • • • • •

Ryan was an emotionally immature 16-year-old. He struggled with transitions, found it difficult to form and maintain friendships, expressed feelings of low self-worth and was not engaging with education. His parents were frustrated with his constant presence in front of the television and lack of motivation. They were very concerned that he would never be able to achieve independence. His loneliness and isolation were impacting on them emotionally and they often felt a sense of despair at his inability to engage in life in the way his peers were.

In exploring Ryan's early history in his birth family a picture emerged of a little boy who had been left alone for long periods of time; his birth mother had had multiple partners who were often violent to her and who humiliated Ryan. His birth mother would often take out her frustrations about her own life on Ryan and when he was eventually placed in foster care at the age of six years he would frequently make statements about being a 'bad boy' and engaged in self-harming behaviours.

Exploration of what was going on for Ryan within his therapeutic work revealed that he was still struggling with profound feelings of low self-worth and shame; these feelings were reinforced by his acute awareness of his difference to his peers. He felt trapped by and 'stuck' in his negative perceptions and expectations of himself. He described his extreme anxiety at the thought of having to register for his new college place. What if he went to the wrong building, what if someone asked him a question he couldn't answer correctly, what if everyone else was ganging up in friendship groups and he was left out as usual? He also reflected on his anxiety about friendships: other kids of his age would tease him and laugh at him, and he always said stupid things and ended up being left out. His awareness of the consequences of not managing the key transitions at this stage of his life only served to increase his anxiety. He was failing again and his whole future was now in jeopardy.

Clearly, Ryan's difficulties in engaging in life were about difficulties that were much more challenging than laziness or indifference. No wonder it felt safer for him to remain in front of the television or his computer console when his anxiety and fears were so overwhelming. A key element of the therapeutic work with his parents was to help them understand the emotional challenges that were driving Ryan's behaviour. His difficulties were reframed as 'can't do' rather than 'won't do'; in response to this understanding, Ryan's parents were able to reframe their approach to supporting him with his difficulties. They put in place a number of supportive strategies that met his needs at his emotional rather than chronological age and recognized his own limited expectations of himself. They engaged the local college in providing a staff mentor who came out to the home to help Ryan with the registration process and answer any questions for him. A lot of structure around his arrival at college, unstructured breaks and lunchtimes were provided. This meant that Ryan had regular check-in points and strategies for what to do if he was feeling particularly anxious. Ryan's parents also helped him to join the local Sea Cadet's group. This highly structured and task-driven activity base enabled Ryan to be a part of a peer group for at least two evenings a week in a way that he could manage. As Ryan took small steps in successfully managing in these key areas of his life, his confidence and enthusiasm gradually improved. It would be a long road for him towards independence but he and his parents could begin to see a future in which he could very slowly move towards more independence.

• •

Pruning, too, may have an impact on young people's susceptibility to low mood and anxiety during adolescence. The adolescent brain goes through an extensive process of pruning as the brain remodels itself and strips away neural networks it no longer needs as it prepares for adult life. To some degree the timing and pace of this process is genetically determined[16] but stress can also accelerate the pruning process and leave insufficient neurons and connections to balance mood effectively. Many adopted young people are experiencing high levels of stress because of their particular vulnerabilities and may therefore be more vulnerable to this acceleration of the pruning process.

Conclusion

The emotional challenges discussed in this chapter are, in my experience, some of the primary emotional struggles that young people often present with when their parents seek support from services. It isn't possible to cover the many examples and variations of circumstances and individual experiences of the many adopted teenagers who require support, but it is hoped the examples given will provide food for thought in thinking about the emotional struggles that may be there for young people underneath their presenting behaviours. Young people will, of course, differ in the way in which their emotional responses are activated. This will depend on the young person's individual personality.

One way to describe personality is that we can have a general tendency to activate one of three major emotional states of distress: fear and anticipatory anxiety, sadness and separation distress, and anger and rage.[17]

Many parents express their feeling that their teenager, caught up in these sometimes overwhelming experiences, is oblivious to the impact that these difficulties have on them as parents. This is understandable, as the young person is often extremely preoccupied by his or her own struggles (Chapter Two explores the downturn in empathy in the teenage brain), but in my experience, young people are greatly impacted and concerned by the impact that their difficulties have on their parents and families even if they can't express this to their parents.

> I kept asking myself 'What's wrong with me?' I felt so angry and I kept having thoughts that really bothered me. Sometimes I'd be crying for no reason, I was really horrible to people, I don't know how anyone stayed liking me. My brother was like, 'You're f****** mental you are.' I felt like I was ruining my family.

I would like to conclude this chapter with an important note about the potential impact of the young people's emotional struggles on their parents' emotional wellbeing. The teenager's emotional struggles will inevitably impact on his or her parent's emotional state and the degree to which the young person struggles emotionally will have a direct correlation with the stress the parent is placed under:

> Just as the teenager feels overwhelmed and out of control the process is paralleled in the parent's experience…[18]

If we are to think of the adopted adolescent's emotional life as containing all of the stresses of 'usual' adolescence but with bells on, we also need to anticipate and accept that the young person's parents may well be experiencing a parallel process. They are having to manage emotional challenges that are 'beyond the norm'. Many of the parents I have worked with find themselves experiencing and struggling with the very emotions that their children are struggling with. When I asked parents to comment on their experiences I received some of the following feedback.

On feeling a sense of shame

I have felt that I am a pretty crap parent at times. Helpless or hopeless; either way I have often felt ashamed. I didn't envisage myself as this kind of parent. I do feel an acute sense of feeling that this is my fault; I'm not doing a good enough job here. Sometimes I feel embarrassed by his difficulties too; that feels like a terrible thing to say.

On feeling angry

Sometimes my anger matches hers. I am angry that this has happened to our family, angry that she went through what she did and sometimes I am angry with her. The pushing and antagonizing feels very personal, I think anyone would need to be superhuman not to react. Afterwards I feel terrible. I do understand that it isn't her fault.

On the confusion it can cause

I did question whether this was just a part of the way in which teenagers are emotionally. I found it quite hard to define why I thought it was 'more than'.

Don't underestimate the impact that living with someone who is depressed (or angry) can have on you. If you aren't careful you can end up in the same place that they are, it's very confusing…you think this isn't who I am!

On low mood, anxiety and the risk of isolation

It can be very lonely parenting a child who just isn't like the children of your friends. It's hard to talk to friends about it because it's just difficult for them 'to get it'. It's hard to do what your friends with teenagers are doing i.e. maybe having a bit more freedom to go out for example. I can't because I'm worrying about her so much. It's a very different experience to other parents.

It is incredibly important that both parents and the professionals who work with them understand that it is impossible to be in the role of caregiver to a young person who is struggling without being deeply impacted by this. I will continue to explore the parents' experiences in the chapters that follow.

BEHAVIOURS AND 'WAYS OF BEING'

Chapter One focused on some of the key emotional themes that can be present for adopted teenagers and the way in which these may emerge in behaviours. This chapter will explore the behaviours that parents often ask for advice about (while considering the emotions that may underpin them). Many of the behaviours discussed are, like the emotional themes in Chapter One, common to the majority of adolescents. As with the emotional themes, although these behaviours may be common to teenagers generally, the behaviours presented by adopted adolescents are different in the intensity and degree to which they are experienced. Some behaviours are very different to the 'usual' range of adolescent behaviours and are specifically related to the impact of early trauma and the young person's development.

In my experience, the behaviours described below, are some of the most common causes of concern for parents (and often for the young people themselves).

Being selfish and lacking in empathy

Parents of adolescents often express concern that aspects of their child's personality change when they enter the adolescent years. Some parents will identify an increase in selfishness and a lack of empathy as one of their primary concerns, worrying that these changes mean that their child is destined to be an adult with poorly developed qualities in these key areas. Parents will identify a range of behaviours that can be particularly frustrating during this time: a lack of willingness to help in the house, a perceived lack of concern for parents' and siblings' wellbeing, an inability/refusal to recognize what parents do for them, a sense of injustice if any requests are made of them and yet a skilled ability to engage in tasks if there is a desired reward within reach!

It is the case that 'normal' development in the teenage brain can lead to an increase in selfish behaviour and reduced capacity for empathy. Empathy is 'a quality in which one person understands the perspective of another, accepts this perspective as belonging to the other person and conveys this understanding and acceptance back to the person.'[1] When we are empathetic we are able to recognize the needs of others, respond to them and often to place the needs of the other before our own. Parents may well experience not inconsiderable frustration at their adolescent's seeming inability to recognize, accept, understand or respond to others' perspectives and needs. A simple request for assistance in completing a chore may be met with protestations of all the unfair demands the parents make on the young person for example, the young person seemingly oblivious to the many considerations the parent feels they provide for their teenage child. Why can teenagers sometimes appear to be so selfish and lacking in empathy? It is useful to bear in mind the quality of mind of 'creative exploration' when answering this question. This quality of mind serves in many ways to create a more intensive focus on the self and drives an increased level of self-exploration and preoccupation for the young person.[2] It is also helpful to think of the various structural changes in the young person's rapidly changing brain as influencing this downturn in empathy.

> During adolescence the brain undergoes huge changes, with a major increase in synaptic connections in the frontal lobes and later a major pruning process. The teenage brain is flooded with hormones, which drive this process, a process that takes control of their bodies and brain simultaneously. Such major brain changes often lead to a downturn in the teenager's level of empathy. The once caring and helpful son or daughter refuses to help with small tasks around the house, and appears to lose any sense of empathy or sympathy for anyone else.[3]

The adopted young person will also have additional emotional challenges during this stage of development leaving less space for the consideration of others. They may therefore seem to be particularly preoccupied with themselves and lacking in empathy (which may well be delayed in terms of development before they reach the teenage years anyway). Adopted adolescents whose brains are less well integrated and potentially vulnerable to excessive pruning may well struggle with empathy more than their peers for these reasons.

The adopted adolescent's refusal to engage in or consider others within family life in this way is also sometimes overlaid with rejecting statements: 'Why should I, you're not my mum anyway.' These statements of rejection can feel particularly hurtful for parents but rarely represent a long-term message of rejection; rather, they are tied up in 'the muddle' of the young person's emotional maelstrom during this stage (I will look to exploring some of the identity dilemmas that may lead to statements like this in Chapter Six). The lack of consideration for others is a developmental state that does not (necessarily!) continue into adulthood. In my experience, it is not usually the case that those adolescents who seem to show a scant regard for their parents' perspective or needs necessarily extend this attitude outside of the home. Teenagers I have worked with have often shown a high level of empathy for their peers who are experiencing difficulties, and indeed many teenagers who have been through their own challenging times are particularly attuned to and motivated to help peers whose difficulties resonate with their own experiences. Adolescents are, of course, often much more concerned with the way in which they are experienced and perceived by their peers and this is very much developmentally appropriate. It may go some way to explaining this differing capacity to demonstrate empathy within home life and the young person's social world!

There are some teenagers who enter adolescence with a very poorly developed capacity for empathy because of earlier experiences of trauma and loss. Poorly integrated prefrontal functions, which help us to have empathy for ourselves and others, place these young people at a disadvantage. Young people who have difficulties in attachment relationships struggle to feel emotionally connected to others. This difficulty means that they struggle to understand their own emotions, to read the emotions of others or to anticipate how another might behave in response to them.[4] These factors can leave them very poorly equipped in the empathy stakes.

Boredom and risk taking

Any parent of a teenager will be familiar with the refrain of: 'I'm bored.' Teenagers do seek a higher level of new and exciting stimulation. The neurological explanation for teenagers' lower tolerance to boredom is likely to be found in the fact that baseline levels of dopamine are lower in the teenage brain (dopamine is the 'feel-good' reward chemical in our brains and can be lower still in teenagers who are struggling emotionally). The release of dopamine in response to experience is higher though during this developmental stage. The adolescent's 'reward system' is firing on all cylinders. The teenager is likely to experience intense surges of 'highs', which then quickly fall again. Teenagers may consequently feel lower in mood ('bored') unless they are being stimulated. The quality of mind of 'novelty seeking'[5] and the corresponding drive to seek new and stimulating activities is also an important feature of teenage life, and it serves a developmental purpose in taking the adolescent out into the wider world to prepare for adult life. Risk taking is incredibly important and can be a very positive feature of teenage life. Adolescents can be innovative, daring, exciting, ground breaking and brave. There are, though, a number of features of the adolescent brain that can mean risk-taking behaviour can be extreme and dangerous for young people.

One of the challenges for teenagers is that while the reward-seeking system may be at full tilt in the teenage years, the prefrontal, monitoring brain is not yet functioning at its full capacity. This means that the thinking processes that can place a pause on impulsive, risk-taking behaviour are not yet 'balancing out' this important drive. Adolescents are also much more likely to anticipate a positive outcome when weighing up risk ('hyper-rational thinking') and this can lead to difficulties: 'hyper-rational thinking considers the impulse and senses the reward drive to realize the positive thrill'.[6]

When weighing up risk, teenagers are much more likely to focus on the chance of success and not the potentially negative consequences of their decisions.

Adopted teenagers may be more likely to engage in worrying levels of risky behaviour because of vulnerabilities they carry as a consequence of their early experiences and the impact of these on their development. Some of these additional vulnerabilities may include the following points.

- Some teenagers may have entered adolescence somewhat behind their peers in their capacity to link cause and effect. Because they are poor at understanding the behaviour of others and have a limited capacity for reflective function, their ability to interpret the behaviour of self and others through an understanding of mental states is compromised.[7]

- Some teenagers will have a poorer capacity to moderate 'lower brain' impulses (which may lead to risk taking).

- Some young people have not had the experience of feeling safe in earlier childhood, which makes judgements in relation to safety and feeling safe very challenging. These young people may have a persistent sense of a lack of safety in the world, and reckless, risky behaviours may be sending a strong message about this.

- Some young people who experienced high levels of stress in early life will have developed a 'baseline' state of arousal that meant they were in a physiological state of high arousal/persistent alarm. They may need to seek intense feeling (higher dopamine hits) because they have developed a degree of 'emotional numbing'.

- Some adolescents may use risk taking and the intense emotional states that go with it to detract from their emotional pain.

- As I discussed in Chapter One, some young people will have a profound lack of self-worth. They may carry a sense of failure in not managing 'mainstream life' in the same way their peers do, leaving them with a feeling of alienation from many of the peers they have grown up with. They may increase risk-taking behaviour as a way of impressing and connecting with peers, and this need and risk-related way of connecting may extend to sexual behaviour (this will be explored further in Chapter Seven). Their sense of hopelessness may also lead them to engage in more reckless behaviour: 'What's the point?'

• Some young people's risk-taking behaviour may be related to identifying with risky behaviours they associate with their birth family. (This element of identity exploration will be explored in Chapter Six.)

Risk-taking behaviour can lead to physical danger to the self and others and even criminal behaviour. Drug taking and excessive alcohol use tends to encompass all of these elements, and parents will often identify this as one of the risk-taking behaviours they worry about the most. Drug and alcohol use can be very much connected to the way in which teenagers socialize, and the reality is that drugs and alcohol are readily available to those who want to use them. Many adolescents regard this aspect of teenage life as merely a fun, experimental and social function. Whilst carrying its own risks, this is, of course, often part of the attraction for adolescents. The adolescent brain, though, is particularly susceptible to addiction, a risk that most young people don't fully appreciate.

> Our changing adolescent brain is especially vulnerable to respond to drug use with the onset of a cascade of behavioral and physiological responses that can contribute to addiction. Such vulnerability to addiction is due to both the activation of certain genes and the altering of neural functioning, making the dopamine release dependent on drug use.[8]

My own experience of working with adopted teenagers is that they can be particularly susceptible to addiction because, as well as the thrill-seeking component, they will sometimes use drugs as a way of self-medicating, a way of changing the way they feel. Unfortunately, whilst self-medicating in this way may initially be experienced as effective in serving its purpose, many young people find that they do then become dependent upon the drug itself for their dopamine (feel-good chemical) release.

• • • • • • • • • • RUTH AGED 15 • • • • • • • • • •

Ruth had experienced profound neglect and physical abuse for the first three years of her life whilst living with her birth mother and older brother. Her environment had been a scary and unpredictable one within which there was little comfort or safety. Ruth had learnt to 'cut off' from her overwhelming emotional states in order to survive. Her tendency to avoid painful emotions and memories had continued throughout her childhood and she had great difficulty in even recognizing her feeling states much of the time. She struggled with sleeping as she often awoke with nightmares and would sometimes find herself crying without being able to identify the trigger for this. She was also hyper vigilant, describing her anxiety about being outside of the home at times and wondering what people were thinking and saying about her. When asked how she was doing, Ruth would always reply 'fine'. She described herself as a happy and bubbly person; indeed she did present in this way a great deal of the time, but she also experienced explosive outbursts that were impacting negatively on her family relationships. Ruth used cannabis a lot and her parents were worried about this. Ruth described her cannabis use as something that was helpful and beneficial for her. She felt that it helped her to sleep, to feel calmer when she was getting angry, stopped her brain from 'going overtime' and generally 'chilled her out' and it helped her to feel good. Ruth did acknowledge that she experienced increased feelings of paranoia and was worried about how much she smoked at times but regarded these as minor side effects in contrast to the perceived benefits. She also pointed out that most of her friends smoked, that they all generally preferred that to drinking and that it was just a part of their everyday lives.

In Ruth's case, cannabis use had the effect of helping to reinforce her avoidance of more painful and challenging feelings and gave her some of that 'feel-good' feeling that she struggled to find in day-to-day life. She was probably accurate in her description of the immediate effects and benefits she felt whilst smoking, but she had increasingly become dependent on cannabis to obtain this feeling. The side effects of increased paranoia, worsening mood swings and ongoing fragmentation was also far from beneficial for her.

Other young people who may gain a perceived sense of comfort and pleasure from maintaining more 'hyper' (rather than 'hypo' states) may be more likely to choose the alcohol and drugs that reinforce those states. Whatever the choice, the risk that dopamine release becomes dependent upon drug use is a very real one for many young people and it is this dependence that may lead them into further risky behaviours in order to maintain the addiction.

Lying, stealing and sabotage: behaviours linked to trauma in young people

Lying and stealing (and indeed sabotage) may not be linked to trauma. Teenagers do lie; for example if they want to circumvent adults' rules, they may steal for a dare (risk taking) or they may sabotage a family outing if they are angry and sulking because they wanted to meet up with friends. Whilst these behaviours may not be particularly desirable, they don't necessarily point to more serious underlying difficulties. Sometimes, though, these behaviours may be related to more complex emotional needs. Some of these are highlighted below.

Lying

Lying can be a significant concern for adoptive parents because of the nature and intensity of lying that some adopted teenagers present with. Parents will often describe 'nonsensical' lying and persistent dishonesty as some of their primary concerns. The potential consequences of this behaviour for the young person's future are worrying for parents. Lying also destroys trust in relationships and parents may feel that it signifies a lack of respect for them on the young person's part as well as a disregard for the relationship. Parents often comment that they feel both betrayed and hurt by lies and insecure in their parental relationship with their child as a consequence of frequent lying.

There may be a number of reasons as to why teenagers lie (outside of the 'normal' range of lying behaviour). For those adolescents with low self-esteem, lying may serve to bolster their sense of self. As adolescents are particularly sensitive to their peers' views and opinions about them, this behaviour may escalate during teenage years. Young people who feel a lot of shame may feel a need to present a 'false front' to their peers, a persona and character that mask their deep-seated sense of self-doubt and dislike of the self.

• • • • • • • • • • • MAX AGED 12 • • • • • • • • • • • •

Max was a deeply insecure young boy. His birth mother had rejected him and he had suffered a second rejection when his first adoptive placement had broken down because his parents had struggled to manage his challenging behaviour. Max was adopted for a second time and benefited from stability within that placement but he remained a highly anxious boy who struggled to trust that he could be lovable. People found Max to be charming and engaging when they first met him. He sought to engage others and would show them his breakdancing skills, talk about how well he was doing at school and show off his karate moves. Max was lively, with a constant chatter. Unfortunately, after some time in his company, adults and particularly peers would start to feel uncomfortable with Max. Max's stories about his achievements would start to feel slightly grandiose, his boasts began to seem disingenuous and his constant chatter left little room for reciprocal interaction. Eventually, Max's desperate need to control other's perceptions of him would lead to further rejection.

Young people who are struggling to make sense of their past may construct their own stories and narratives to try and create a sense of security in defining themselves. Sometimes these may be idealized versions of their lives in order that they can avoid the painful reality.

• • • • • • • • • • SARAH AGED 13 • • • • • • • • •

Sarah found it very difficult to think about the reality of her early life in her birth family where she had been seriously neglected. She had loved her birth parents, who could be nurturing and gave her very powerful messages about the importance of birth family and identity. She had been adopted when she was seven years old. In trying not to acknowledge the reality of her past and her painful feelings she had constructed an alternative narrative about her history to protect herself. She would explain that she was removed from her birth parents because of neglect but that it probably wasn't their fault: 'The shops weren't open so they couldn't buy food/they didn't have enough money, we didn't have beds because there weren't any bed shops where we lived, my mum was just fun she liked to have parties…'

Some young people may tell lies that represent a version of their lives that they wish were real. Others may lie in response to overwhelming feelings of shame; the lie is much safer than feeling 'I am bad at my very core.' Sometimes lies serve to keep a distance between the young person and their parents; those young people who don't like adults to get 'too close' can be very skilled at keeping them at a distance through undesirable behaviour (anger keeps a relationship at a distance too for example). Sometimes lies serve to bring others closer; young people who struggle to identify and articulate the reason for unmet emotional need may construct a lie to provide a reason for evoking sympathy and nurture from others. Some teenagers may have a fragile grasp on reality: they may still be immature in their development or may have experienced a childhood in which adults consistently lied, were unreliable or failed to be transparent.[9] The stressed teenage brain, which is experiencing too much pruning and is busy firing from the amygdala without the balance of sufficient cortical reasoning, may not have the best grasp on reality. Adopted teenagers who are delayed in the development of empathy (or whose empathy capacity is lower during this stage) may not fully appreciate the impact of their lies on others.

Whilst parents' concerns in relation to lying are entirely understandable, it is important to remember that at the route of lying are many different needs. Identifying and untangling what is driving the teenager's need to lie can be helpful in reducing this behaviour. This will be addressed further in the following chapter.

Stealing

Stealing, like lying, can serve a number of purposes. If a young person has a poorly developed sense of conscience and empathy, he or she may steal without grasping the impact that this may have on others. They steal because they want something and don't comprehend the potential impact of this on relationships. They may also have a poorly developed grasp of cause and effect. As discussed above, adolescents are also likely to balance risk in a different way and so are more likely to assess the chances of getting away with stealing as being balanced in their favour.

Some young people may steal because they carry a sense of resentment and injustice about what they haven't had in their earlier lives: 'Why shouldn't I have this?' Young people who were neglected in their early development may be trying to fill a sense of emptiness/absence of something; this behaviour can feel like a need that can't be met, a sense of 'I need it' without really knowing what they need. Many young people will have had to scavenge for food in their early lives; taking food and other items would have been a case of survival. As adolescents experience higher levels of anxiety they may revert to earlier behaviours, unconsciously aware of the emotional needs driving these behaviours. Stealing and hoarding can also be a strategy for managing anxiety; the adolescent may be seeking to gather resources that will make them feel more secure. Like lying, stealing can serve to keep relationships at a distance. Some teenagers may also unconsciously steal to provoke anger in parents in order to discharge anger/seek conflict.[10] Some adolescents may steal in order to seek approval from peers, either to impress or for the shared sense of risk (and consequent dopamine hit!), or as a way of attempting to please peers in giving them gifts.

Sabotage

Young people who sabotage potentially positive experiences may do so for a number of reasons. Teenagers with low self-worth may feel that they are not worthy of pleasant experiences; they may struggle with new situations or social situations or fear that it will go wrong anyway and so hasten the inevitable along.

• • • • • • • • • • • DARREN AGED 14 • • • • • • • • • • •

Ryan had been adopted into a large and loving family when he was four years old. Ryan's extended family was full of aunts, uncles and cousins who his parents liked to socialize with. Ryan, though, was a highly anxious teenager who struggled to express his needs. He struggled with transitions and was socially awkward and shy; these difficulties had escalated in his teenage years as he became more aware of himself in relation to others. Before social events Ryan would either refuse to leave the house with his parents, stating that he didn't feel well or didn't feel like it, or he inevitably seemed to create conflict. He and his parents would end up arguing and he would refuse to go out with them, blaming them for ruining his mood. Ryan's parents were frustrated and disappointed by the seemingly puzzling changes in Ryan's personality. What they hadn't realized was that Ryan felt overwhelmed by anxiety within social situations; his behaviour was a communication of his inability to manage these situations rather than a desire to sabotage these relationships and opportunities for time with his wider family.

• •

Young people who are full of anger may sabotage situations as a way 'getting back' at parents, when they are unable to express this in any other way. This section can only cover these quite complex themes relatively briefly. I would particularly recommend Caroline Archer's books, *First Steps in Parenting the Child Who Hurts* and *Next Steps in Parenting the Child Who Hurts,* as very useful texts in thinking about these themes.[11]

Self-harm

Self-harm may be a way in which the adolescent tries to seek attention from others; it may be an expression of need for nurture and care. Adopted teenagers may be particularly susceptible to trying to gain their need for care in this way because they are not very good at signalling their attachment needs. An insecure-avoidant adolescent, for example, may not be aware of or easily able to express their more painful feelings because they do not anticipate that adults can meet their emotional needs (the difficulties that can emerge from insecure attachment styles are discussed in Chapter Five). Self-harm may also be a way of avoiding unwanted distressing feelings; physical pain can feel more concrete and manageable. Alternatively, self-harm may also be a way of releasing overwhelming feelings of anger and frustration. Adopted adolescents may, again, be more vulnerable to experiencing feelings that seem overwhelming because their emotional experience may be so much more complex and intense during this stage.

Controlling behaviour
• • • • • • • • • • MEGAN AGED 16 • • • • • • • • • •

Megan's early life within her birth family had been chaotic. Her birth mother moved around frequently, often taking Megan with her to friends' houses where she would get high. Megan often had to fend for herself. Megan drove her adoptive mother to distraction. She would check on her movements whilst she was at school, sending her numerous texts to ask where she was and what she was doing. She would question her decisions and dominate conversations when visitors came to the home. Megan would try to control all of the choices at home: what they ate for dinner, when her mum should go to bed and which television programmes they should watch.
• •

Very controlling behaviour can be wearying for parents to manage. Controlling behaviours have often been present for young people in earlier childhood but can escalate or emerge during the adolescent years. The need to control the world around them is often a feature of children's behaviour when they are highly anxious and have difficulties in trusting adults to keep them safe or meet their emotional needs. Adopted adolescents may increase their controlling behaviours for a number of reasons. In the teenage years, young people will become more aware of the lack of control that they have had in their earlier lives. Social services, the courts and other professionals made decisions that affected their lives profoundly. They may be keenly aware of the way in which those decisions continue to impact on their lives, particularly in relation to the access they can or can't have to their files, restrictions and boundaries around contact arrangements and so on. Autonomy is a key theme in adolescence and it can take on an urgency and value for young people who haven't had control over events and decisions that have so impacted their lives in their childhoods to date. Teenagers struggling with the balance of control in their present (as they push against their parents' boundaries) may feel an increased sense of injustice because of the lack of control they have experienced in many other ways. It is important to acknowledge, too, that the physiological changes for young people in adolescence can feel scary and 'out of control'. Adopted teenagers may particularly struggle with the onset of puberty and its very visible physical signs of moving out of childhood when they are not yet ready for this emotionally.

These young people, too, have missed out on the critical first year of experiencing being loved unconditionally without yet having to experience discipline and conditions on their behaviour. Adoptive parents can really struggle to help their children develop trust in them because they have missed this important stage.

A note about sleep and underlying emotional states

Teenagers' sleep patterns do change. Whilst adolescents need more sleep than adults, it is also recognized that they fall asleep later than their parents and wake up later. This may be because melatonin (the 'sleep chemical') is released later in the evening for teenagers than it is for younger children or adults. Whilst the changes in teenagers' sleep patterns can be frustrating for all parents, there can be additional difficulties for young people who have experienced early trauma in getting to sleep. Many young people who have been removed from their birth families will not have had nurturing, supported bedtime routines in their early years. They may have been left to sleep wherever they lay down or they may have had extremely frightening experiences because of domestic violence incidents in the evening or night-time. Many young children will have been in households where unsafe adults were in the home and sometimes in the children's bedrooms. All young children need support in making the transition to bedtime; if this isn't provided and in addition the night-time is a source of fear and unpredictability, the impact of this can be felt throughout childhood.

> Sleep requires a reduction in arousal levels. As bedtime can exacerbate trauma based stress responses such as: fear of abandonment, triggers for abusive experiences, as well as early established patterns in remaining alert to signals of violence, the opportunity to forage for food and so on, the adopted teenager can experience additional difficulties in getting to sleep for many reasons.[11]

As teenagers are likely to fall asleep later than their parents, they may struggle with the feeling of being alone, particularly when they are trying to defend against anxiety-provoking feelings. Those teenagers who struggle to get to sleep, will often try to fill this time with activities that occupy them and give them a sense of stimulation and comfort. For some adolescents, this may be computer games, talking with their friends on social media or seeking the attention of their parents (positive or negative!). Other young people may seek stimulation outside of the home with other young people who are of a similar mind. The seeking of dopamine can, of course, lead to risk-taking behaviours that propel the teenager outside of the home at exactly the time when he or she is likely to be least safe. The effects of insufficient sleep time also impact on many other areas including: concentration (and ability to focus at school), mood regulation and physical health. Supporting teenagers in being able to get enough sleep and, reducing anxiety and arousal levels in order to be able to sleep in the first place is important. Ideas in supporting this will be discussed in Chapter Three.

Conclusion

As with the emotional challenges discussed in Chapter One, these behaviours are, in my experience, some of the concerning behaviours that young people will present with when their parents seek support from services. Again, it isn't possible to cover the many variations of behaviours and experiences of adopted teenagers, but it is hoped these examples will resonate with parents and provide some context for their experiences. These behaviours do, of course, evoke feelings of fear, distrust, helplessness, confusion, anger and often shame for the parents who are trying to manage them. The next chapter will look to approaches and strategies in beginning to address some of the themes.

Chapter Three

APPROACHES AND STRATEGIES FOR MANAGING THE EMOTIONAL ROLLERCOASTER

The preceding chapters have outlined some of the complexities of the emotional and behavioural challenges that adopted teenagers may present with during this stage of development. This complexity means that it is not possible to provide a 'one-solution-fits-all' argument in meeting and addressing these needs. However, in this chapter, I hope to outline some useful principles, approaches and strategies that may be helpful in meeting the adopted teenager's emotional needs. In meeting their emotional needs, we can, in turn, influence the young person's behaviour. Many of these approaches have been recommended by parents when reflecting on their experiences of parenting. Some of these suggestions may seem useful and appropriate; others may not resonate with your particular circumstances. My hope is that all parents will be able to take something from the ideas discussed that will feel useful to them. In this chapter, I will also discuss some of the important messages for parents in taking care of the self and the value of this in parenting effectively during this time. Further approaches and strategies are also discussed in the chapters that follow.

A useful starting point

The preceding chapters highlighted some of the features and challenges of teenage life that are common themes within 'normal' adolescence and also those that are more specific to adolescence that is impacted by trauma and loss. Understanding that some of the emotional ups and downs of teenage life are both developmentally very appropriate and unavoidable can be helpful. Parents often question whether they are doing something wrong if their child is struggling. Understanding any teenager's struggles as being part of important neurological changes that serve crucial developmental functions, and of a developmental process, is useful in placing the stressful times in context as part of a transitional process. It will not remain this way forever! It is also helpful to think of the adopted teenager's particular struggles as emanating from a complex combination of the impact of their early experiences as well as the 'usual teenage stuff'. The adopted adolescent's emotional journey may be more complex and much more challenging, but these particular difficulties, too, are part of a process and can provide an opportunity for complex emotional needs to be met. The intensity and nature of the difficulties that arise during this time are not static in nature and, if parents are able to respond to the underlying emotional needs during this time, the young person can emerge from adolescence having overcome some significant challenges.

If we think of behaviour as a communication of the young person's emotional inner world we can place ourselves in a useful position as 'emotional detectives'. Whilst the emotions driving the adopted teenager's behaviours will inevitably be more complex and perhaps less easily decipherable, they do provide smoke signals that can give clues to the adolescent's internal struggles. The case studies in the previous chapter provided some examples of how addressing the emotional needs underneath behaviours can help to decrease some of the more worrying behaviours we may see in adolescents.

This chapter will continue with a focus on the principle that we must first meet the young person's emotional needs if we are to have an impact on behaviour. In doing so I will explore the following areas: the value of the parent–child relationship; the value of play and fun times; the importance of taking care of oneself; the value of repair; and the stance of PACE (playfulness, acceptance, curiosity and empathy) as an overarching approach.

Consideration will also be given to: useful strategies for particular behaviours; the question of boundaries and consequences; and managing risk. The positive value of all of these principles and approaches as promoting positive integration of the brain will also be discussed.

The value of maintaining the parent–child relationship

One of the most important messages for parents in supporting their adopted teenager with emotional challenges and difficult behaviours is that maintaining the attachment relationship is of huge value. This is one of the most protective factors for young people's emotional health.

In *Helping Teenagers with Anger and Low Self-Esteem* Margot Sunderland describes the positive benefits for the adolescent brain when the parent–child relationship is a good one.[1] A good relationship means that the teenage brain will activate optimal levels of opioids and oxytocin, not all the time but enough to maintain a generally positive state of mind. These biochemicals are anti-anxiety, anti-aggression chemicals. They are a protective factor against aggressive, difficult behaviour escalating. Conversely, if there is a lot of conflict within the parent–child relationship, stress chemicals are prevalent and feelings of anger, depression and anxiety are more likely to be triggered. Poor relationships can also increase risk-taking behaviour. In short, good chemicals equal a calmer and healthier brain. This is an important message for parents because sometimes it can seem very difficult to find a reason to 'hang on in there' when relationships have become very strained because of the young person's behaviour.

I am not suggesting, of course, that it is possible for parents to maintain a good relationship with their teenage child at all times. Parents cannot help but respond to the extreme stresses that can be present as a result of their child's emotional struggles. The parent often bears the brunt of the young person's distress, anger and frustration:

> But because teenagers are often rude, provocative, dismissing and abusive to parents, it is easy to see how negative patterns of relating are very common in parent–child relationships. In fact, responding effectively to an angry, sulky or violent teenager is a real art, requiring a lot of complex and sophisticated skills, which don't tend to come naturally.[2]

It is difficult to overstate just how challenging this can be at times for parents. Wanting and being able to maintain a relationship with a child who seems intent on either rejecting, hurting, punishing, dismissing or being excessively demanding of the parent can feel absolutely overwhelming at times. Parents may sometimes find themselves thinking (and sometimes saying): 'Why should I?', 'What's the point?', 'Nothing I am doing is working' or 'I haven't made a bit of difference to him/her anyway so I may as well just give in.' A strong desire to distance oneself from a very stressful relationship is understandable; it's a protective strategy in the face of very painful emotional experiences. Conversely, some parents may find themselves increasingly entrenched in 'the battle', moving further and further into conflict in an attempt to take some control over the relationship. Whatever the parent's individual response, when these reactions become defensive and reactive to the young person's dysregulated state, very little space for nurturing and attuned parenting can be left within the relationship. This, in turn, leaves scant opportunity for the good protective chemicals that promote the calmer, healthier brain.

In order to maintain a positive relationship with their teenager, it is important for parents to remain as emotionally healthy and regulated as possible. Overwhelming levels of stress can impact on our capacity to be an effective parent. An excellent exploration of the 'parenting brain' can be found in *Brain-Based Parenting* by Hughes and Baylin.[3] Professionals working with families often give focus to the impact of trauma and stress on the child's developing brain, but it is equally important to recognize that parents' brains are also impacted by stress in the present and trauma and stress emanating from their own childhood experiences.

Paying attention to the 'parenting brain'

Parenting a traumatized child has a profound impact on a parent's experience and wellbeing. This is considered more fully in Chapter Nine, but I would like to focus here on the impact of stress on the 'parenting brain' and what it means in relation to a parent's ability to parent across the domains of caregiving highlighted by Hughes and Baylin.

When we experience high levels of stress as parents our capacity to provide attuned and effective care for our children can be impeded. Our 'emotional' brains are strongly activated and our higher cognitive capacities for self-regulation, self-awareness and empathy 'are not as well connected'.[4] This 'blocked care' (a reduced capacity to provide caregiving) can occur for parents for a number of reasons. Sometimes parents may struggle to parent their child effectively because of challenges that arise at particular developmental stages, such as adolescence. Young people are often less receptive to their parents' care during this time and this can trigger feelings of rejection for parents, leaving them feeling defensive. Parenting adopted teenagers may leave parents particularly vulnerable to these feelings because of the way in which adopted young people may struggle with attachment relationships during this stage (this area is explored further in Chapter Five).

Blocked care may also occur because of specific challenges in parenting the young person or because of difficulties in the parent's own past. Blocked care can occur across the following domains of caregiving in the parenting brain.

- The parental approach system which enables parents to be close to their child without becoming defensive.

- The parental reward system which makes it possible for the parent to experience pleasure from parenting.

- The parental meaning making system which allows the parent to construct a working narrative or story about being a parent.

- The parental child reading system which supports the ability of the parent to understand and empathize with a child's inner subjective experiences.

- The parental executive system, the brain system that relies on the higher brain regions and helps the parent to regulate the lower more automatic brain responses. The executive system helps parents to monitor their own feelings and actions, as well as the state of attunement or misattunement with their child. This system is also crucial for resolving conflicts between parental and unparental feelings, and reflecting on our experiences of being a parent. The parental executive system, heavily dependent on the functioning of the frontal lobes, helps to keep the other four systems 'on' and 'working'.[5]

Asking questions that may reflect difficulties in blocked care can be useful as a 'health check' for your own wellbeing.

- Am I able to feel close to my child?

- Am I able to gain any pleasure from parenting at the moment?

- How do I feel about being a parent? Do I feel that I am failing as a parent? Do I understand why I am responding in the way I am?

- Am I able to understand what is going on for my child? Am I able to understand the emotions underneath the behaviours? Can I feel any empathy for my child?

- Am I able to resolve conflicts within the relationship? Can I regulate my own feelings within this? Do I find myself 'flipping out' too often?

Parents are likely to experience blocked care at some points in their child's adolescence but if they identify that they are experiencing difficulties across these areas in a chronic way it is likely that they will need support.

When blocked care is developmentally stage specific

There may be an indication that a parent is experiencing stage-specific blocked care if they find themselves responding strongly to changes in the young person that are actually very appropriate for this stage of development. Strong feelings of rejection in response to a young person's decreasing need for caregiving at times, which may result in a parent being less available emotionally, can be distressing for both the parent and the young person. Feeling rejected and offended that a teenage child questions one's value systems may lead to a reduced capacity to openness in parenting too. Parenting in adolescence years does require parents to be flexible in expectations and to adapt from their previous parenting role. It is useful, in protecting oneself in this area, to be aware of the changes that occur in adolescence and why. Adolescence does raise complex feelings for parents, and these are valid, but placing them within the context of the developmental stage can help to reduce anxiety and increase understanding of them not as a personal attack but as part of an appropriate process. It can be useful to reflect on one's own adolescence and the influences that have formed our expectations as a parent when we are considering our feelings in this area. This is, of course, much more complex for adoptive parents as the developmentally appropriate changes that occur in adolescence within the parent–child relationship are often experienced with a different degree of complexity and intensity (this is discussed more fully in Chapter Five). The adopted adolescent's teenage behaviours may bear no relation to their parent's experience of adolescence and expectations of this in their own child. For this reason it is particularly important for adoptive parents to be aware of the impact of trauma and loss on adopted young people's adolescent journey. This is why it is also particularity important for adoptive parents to connect with other adoptive parents (this is explored in Chapter Nine).

When blocked care is child specific

The preceding chapters have highlighted a number of ways in which adopted teenagers may create blocked care for their parents. Their particular challenges may mean that they find it challenging to be in the parent–child relationship and this is likely to impact on parents across all of the parenting domains.

When this may be due to the parent's own vulnerabilities

No one has a perfect childhood and most parents will carry their own vulnerabilities (as well as strengths) into their parenting role. These vulnerabilities are much more likely to be triggered when parenting children with their own challenges. The combination of these can be overwhelming and when overwhelmed we can become immersed in implicit triggers, responses and memories.

• • • • • • • • • • • ‹ SARAH › • • • • • • • • • • •

Sarah and her partner adopted a son (Marcus) aged seven years. Max had experienced a great deal of trauma in his early life. His birth mother had neglected him and been punitive and emotionally cruel. She had been unable to recognize his physical or emotional needs and Max had developed a highly avoidant strategy in managing this relationship. Max hid his emotional needs in order to keep his parent close; his internal working model told him that if he expressed his needs the parent may leave and he had no expectation that those needs could be met.

Sarah had had a difficult childhood of her own. Although she had grown up within her birth family, her own mother had suffered from depression and had consequently been flat and unresponsive to Sarah's emotional needs. Sarah had learnt to be self-sufficient from an early age. She found it difficult to identify or express her own needs but was proud that, despite her early difficulties, she had succeeded in life and had formed a long-term supportive relationship with her partner. Initially, when Max was first placed with Sarah and her partner, he had been a compliant child who rarely showed any distress or made any demands of his mum. As Max began to feel safer in his new home though, his emotional demands began to increase. Max couldn't express these needs clearly but he became increasingly oppositional and distressed at even the smallest triggers. Sarah found this very difficult to cope with. She expressed concern that she felt angry in response to Max's distress and her partner saw Sarah as trying to 'shut down' this distress. As Sarah explored what was happening for her within parent support sessions, she reflected on the belief that she carried from her own experiences that the best way to deal with difficult feelings was to 'get on with it'. To stay with these feelings (for her) posed a risk of wallowing in them and by implication becoming overwhelmed by them. Sarah looked at her success in life as being based on her ability to manage by herself and not have to rely too much on others. The difficulty was that in communicating this (however unintentionally) to Max she was unable to support him in expressing his emotional needs and was unable to meet these needs. As a consequence, Max was increasingly dysregulating; he needed support to recognize his emotional needs and to experience a parent who could meet them safely. With support, Sarah was able to reflect on her childhood and understand that she had missed out on rather than gained from the lack of attuned parenting in her early years. Although she had achieved much in many ways in her life, her own emotional life had been compromised by her early experiences. In becoming a parent to a son who desperately needed support in developing a more secure attachment style (his previously avoidant strategies were no longer sustainable), her own vulnerabilities had become more apparent.

• • • • • • • • • • • • • KRIS • • • • • • • • • • • • •

Kris was struggling with parenting his 13-year-old daughter. She was a young person who had angry outbursts and was often physically aggressive. On one occasion Kris had smacked her across the face. Kris felt terrible; he recognized that he had lost control and was seeking help in managing his daughter's behaviour. In reflecting on his own childhood, Kris explained that he had grown up witnessing domestic violence between his mother and father. His parents had argued a lot and he recalled how anxious he used to feel in returning from school, not knowing whether his parents would be OK that evening or if there would be explosive rows. Kris recalled how his heart rate used to increase and his hands would sweat as he approached his home. In exploring how he felt in his body when his daughter was angry, Kris realized that he was experiencing the same 'early warning' signs in preparing for danger as he had as a child. He was effectively moving into fight and flight; his daughter's anger felt overwhelming and was triggering his own early trauma. As Kris continued to explore these early connections he was able to place the feelings triggered by his daughter 'where they belonged', to practise strategies in recognizing his 'early warning' responses and, with the support of his wife, to regulate his responses more easily.

• •

It is incredibly important for parents to be able to reflect on and make sense of the impact of their own childhoods in parenting traumatized children; our own attachment styles have a very real impact on the way in which our neural pathways fire in response to our children's distress:

> Recent brain-imaging studies comparing the brain reactions of parents with secure and insecure adult attachments show intriguing differences, particularly in their brain activity when listening to recordings of their children crying. Whereas the securely attached parents appeared to activate

their reward pathways in response to these sounds of distress, the insecurely attached parents showed a more complicated pattern of brain activity in which they appear to be activating conflicting systems of approach and avoidance.[6]

The benefits of addressing our own vulnerabilities have a direct impact on our children's wellbeing.[7]

The above describes the benefits of self-reflection and exploration, and I believe that specifically focused parent support work should be an integral part of any adoption support provision for families. The importance of supporting parents in order that they are effectively able to support their children's complex emotional needs is discussed more fully in Chapter Nine.

What if parents get it wrong?

Parents are going to get it wrong at times; this is inevitable when managing and responding to such complex emotional needs. Parents often express a huge amount of guilt about the times when they haven't managed situations well or have missed signs/misunderstood their child's particular emotional needs. What is important and very valuable in these instances is the process of repairing mistakes and reconnecting with the young person within this. For the majority of adopted teenagers, the impact of adults' mistakes in their early childhood was catastrophic. Families broke down permanently because parents were unable to 'repair' their mistakes or maintain the relationship with the child. The fact that the young person's relationship with their adoptive parents can survive despites significant stresses is a positive message. It is a message that the child's difficulties are not overwhelming for the parent and that the relationship can survive. Repair, does of course, need to take place once emotions are calmed. When we are upset or angry we are not able to use our 'top-down' cognitive reasoning and reflection skills. Our adult brains are (usually) much more able to make repairs than the adolescent's more immature brains. For this reason, it is often important that parents (with their superior integrated executive systems) lead the process of repair. Adolescents are often increasingly able to do this as they move through adolescence, but it is important to hold on to the value of repair and the reflective opportunities that this provides, even if it is the last thing the frustrated and hurt parent feels like doing! In modelling repair and providing the opportunity for reflection, parents are helping their young person to develop the capacity to do the same.

A note on the distinctive value of parenting in itself

In the case studies in the previous chapter, the parents' investment in the relationships and desire to help their child was also a powerful force in ensuring that they received the support they needed. Their resilience in not giving up and in loving their child despite the difficulties is something that I have been humbled by many times. The nature of the parenting relationship in adoption (and I am not discounting the huge commitment provided in other family arrangements such as special guardianship and long-term foster care), the degree of emotional investment, the desire to keep it positive and the sense of long-term investment in it are things that can be lacking for young people in some care arrangements. This focus on relationship in adoption is absolutely crucial for teenagers in adolescence. The attention to preserving the relationship as a lifelong one is a very powerful message for young people who are adopted.

The use of PACE in promoting a positive relationship

In *Nurturing Attachments*, Golding describes Dan Hughes'[8] model of: playfulness, acceptance, curiosity and empathy (PACE). This model was initially devised as a part of therapy for children with attachment difficulties but it is useful for parents to develop this approach as a habitual way of relating to their child. Golding summarizes the approach:

> Through an attitude of acceptance and empathy the parent is able to co-regulate the child's emotional state. This leads to an improved ability in the child for emotional regulation; she is able to manage her feelings. Through an attitude of curiosity and wondering, the parent is available to co-construct meaning with the child. This helps the child to develop the capacity for reflective function; she is better able to make sense of her experience.[9]

If we look back to the case studies in Chapters One and Two we can see how parents were supported in doing this for their teenagers. Jessica's and Kieran's parents were supported to be curious about what was happening for the young people emotionally (underneath the presenting behaviours), doing so helped them to accept why the young people were behaving as they were (accepting the emotion is different to condoning the behaviours), understanding the reality of the very vulnerable feelings underneath the behaviours helped the parents to be empathetic with their children and in doing this they were able to attune to their child (be with their child in their emotional states and really convey an understanding of this for them). The impact of this for the young people was to help them make sense of their experiences and regulate their own previously overwhelming feelings more easily. Addressing the young people's emotional needs directly impacted on their behaviours. The playful aspect of PACE was not so present in these particular case studies but acceptance, curiosity and empathy certainly were. Love, too, was also very present within the relationships. Further examples of PACE will be evident in case studies throughout the following chapters.

The PACE stance also promotes a positive experience of intersubjectivity in relationships for young people. This can help teenagers to: regulate their emotional experiences more easily, increase their capacity for empathy and reduce their need for control within relationships. Intersubjectivity describes how we are experienced in relationships: if we are understood, our experience is shared (whether this is a joyful experience or a sad one) and empathized with and our emotional needs are met we learn to understand that the influence of others on us can be a positive experience – that we can trust others and that they will understand us. We also learn that others can experience our influence on them and that we can influence how they feel. If we are able to have the experience that our parent (or another significant attachment figure) can think about what we may be feeling and thinking, we begin to understand that we can do that for others too. This also describes the concept of 'mind mindedness'.

Young people can develop their capacity for empathy if they can understand their impact on others' emotional states, and they can reduce their need for control within relationships if they can trust that another have an influence on them can be a positive thing.

Responding to key emotional states: loss, anger, shame and low mood/anxiety

I return to the approach of PACE, particularly acceptance, curiosity and empathy, as the most useful approach in responding to key emotional themes. Acceptance of the fact that adopted adolescents may experience additional challenges in these areas is an important starting point. Being curious about the emotional states underlying behaviours means that we can begin the task of 'making sense' of the young person's challenges in order that we can support them in this. Accepting that often very painful emotional states underlie challenging behaviours helps us to retain our empathy for young people.

Having a good awareness of the teenager's early experiences is important. Parents may not have looked at the early information they received about their child's experiences for a long time; if parents do have information available it is worth revisiting it. If you feel that there are gaps in the information it is worth approaching the post-adoption team for the local authority your children were placed by to request more information from their files. If you have your young person's story in your mind you can be alert to themes that may arise for them and be prepared in advance to be able to 'make sense' of behaviours (smoke signals) that may indicate they are struggling with any of these emotional themes. I use the term 'smoke signals' to describe the types of behaviours that I discuss because the behaviours are usually signalling a difficulty somewhere but the source of this may not be immediately distinguishable. Not all young people can consciously remember their traumatic experiences. Some teenagers might have memories that are explicit: 'I used to get really frightened because my dad hit my mum and I used to hide under the table.' Others will only have implicit memories that are evident in their responses in the present, for example the young person who is still startled in response to police sirens or raised voices. Making the link between the teenager's struggles and responses in the present and their early life events is easier if parents have their early stories in mind.

Reminding yourself of your child's very early experiences is also extremely helpful in helping you to retain empathy for their difficulties.

Life-story work undertaken with the support of a professional within a wider therapeutic context can be very valuable and sometimes it will be absolutely necessary for families who are really struggling. Life story work refers to the process of supporting the young person to understand their own unique history and the impact that this has had on their development and their unique sense of identity. The majority of adopted young people will have received information to support them with this when they were first placed with their adoptive families (for example, a life story book and perhaps a 'later in life letter'). Life story work provides a further expansion of this process in line with the young person's developmental needs (this is discussed further in later chapters). I do think that there is huge value in life-story work being an ongoing process via conversations with the parent throughout the young person's childhood and particularly in teenage years (when the quality of mind of creative exploration means that it can be used particularly well). This does not have to be an intensive process but rather a 'drip, drip' effect of taking opportunities when they arise to make meaning of behaviour for the young person directly, to model a curiosity about what makes us who we are. 'Making meaning of behaviour' is a process that supports the young person to understand why they may be behaving in a certain way, to understand the emotional need that underlies behaviour. As parents, you will know your child better than anybody else. You will know when they are likely to be more open to reflection and, indeed, when they can tolerate empathy! Sometimes teenagers will feel too vulnerable to cope with attention being directed to their own experience and all you may be able to do is model the PACE stance in thinking about others in this way. An example of this may be to comment on television programmes where emotional themes may arise (I have noticed with teenagers I have worked with that they often have a fascination with Jeremy Kyle, possibly because he touches on many themes relevant to their lives!). Verbalizing your awareness of and 'making sense' of other relationships and behaviours involving other people can be useful in aiding the teenager's awareness of the emotions underlying behaviours.

Verbalizing and modelling PACE when it's not focused directly on the young person's experience

The statements below may be useful examples in thinking about 'opening lines' in promoting discussion that includes elements of PACE with the young person.

- 'I wonder what was going on for [name] when they reacted like that.'

- 'Sometimes I think that people are just feeling really sad when they get so angry.'

- 'He said he wasn't bothered about what happened but I think he probably was because I noticed that he: went really quiet/did look quite sad/seemed to want to leave really quickly... I think he finds it really difficult to show how he feels, maybe it's because...'

- 'I'm really sorry that I snapped at you like that earlier; I wasn't actually annoyed at you I was feeling really fed up about...'

The idea is to provide the opportunity for the young person to think about and explore the feelings that may influence behaviours.

Verbalizing and modelling PACE with a focus on the young person's experience

The statements below might be helpful in thinking about discussions with the young person.

- 'You know, I was thinking when you got angry yesterday and we had a row that actually you might have been really worried about…'

- 'I was wondering whether you were a bit upset earlier, I know you said you were fine but I realized that you were really quiet all afternoon. Is there anything I can do to help?'

It may be possible to explore further with the young person by reflecting on your awareness of their particular adaptive responses to their early childhood experiences, which in itself will be very valuable for them.

- 'I sometimes wonder if you find change very difficult because you had so many changes when you were little.'

- 'I have wondered whether you find it really hard to trust that I will look after you and do what I say I'm going to do because you just didn't have adults who did that for you in the past.'

This may also provide the potential to plan for potential difficulties.

- 'We are going to [place] later. I know you find it really difficult when we go to new places and get very anxious so I was wondering about how I could help and make it easier for you?'

- 'I know you find it really hard to let me know when you are worried but I really want to be able to take care of you.

I was thinking that maybe I could guess for you if I think you are having a hard time and you could let me know if I'm right or not?'

Another step beyond this is to link the young person's responses 'in the now' to their early experiences.

- 'I know you find it really difficult to let me know when you are upset because when you were little adults didn't help you when you were unhappy and frightened.'

- 'I know that you find it really hard to trust that I can make good decisions for you. When you were younger adults didn't make good decisions for you. I understand why you would feel safer if you could be in control. I understand that it's because adults caused you harm when you were younger, they didn't get it right.'

Please remember that these are only examples to illustrate possibilities that may be open to you in using this approach; you will be able to judge what feels comfortable or possible in relation to your teenager. It is, of course, important to bear in mind that this approach will only work when the young person is calm and individual teenagers will have differing capacities to receive this. It may be that in your particular circumstances you will need professional support, but helping teenagers with their internal emotional world and making sense of this in relation to their experiences is important.

Clinician's accounts (e.g. Rustin 2006; Hopkins 2006; Right 2009) of working with children highlight the importance of the internal world of the child and in particular the child's search for a coherent account of their life and origins. Lack of attention to the child's grief and loss and incomplete or misunderstood histories are thought to play an important part in the child's inability to develop an integrated sense of self and be associated with disruption.[10]

The value of play in adolescence

The value of 'playfulness' is highlighted within the PACE approach as recognizing the value of being playful in interactions. When parents can experience their teenager in a pleasurable way, laugh together and enjoy lighter moments, this is very valuable for the relationship. Not only is the young person (and parent) receiving some of those positive hormones being released in these moments but he or she is also having an experience of being lovable, enjoyable and able to influence others in a positive way. 'Play' in a wider sense is also important in adolescence. Do teenagers still play? Yes, I think they do and I think that it is useful for parents to think of play in the widest sense when looking for moments when they can connect with their teenage child in positive ways. If it is possible to find activities to enjoy together it will benefit the relationship. One father I worked with recently had found that his son was happy to go to golf practice with him, another mother found that her daughter was open to shared pampering at the nail salon (not exactly 'play' but certainly a pleasurable, relaxing activity that they could share together). This is also beneficial for keeping the 'parenting brain' in good shape and open to the relationship with the young person in the face of challenges. Dopamine neurons fire in our brains even when we are anticipating positive interaction with our children. Hughes and Baylin write that:

> One of the most intriguing findings in research on the parenting brain is that interacting with offspring powerfully activates the brain's reward system (Fleming *et al.*, 2008). The reward system is heavily tied to the chemical dopamine,

which is released into the nucleus accumbens when something pleasurable is encountered in life, including drugs of abuse. Once the dopamine system learns about a good thing, it stores memory of it and then fires in anticipation of having the rewarding experience again. Research shows that our reward system is turned on by interacting with our children. This is an extremely important process that helps to ensure that we will stay engaged and highly motivated to care for our kids.[11]

It is also worth bearing in mind that the emotional intensity of adolescence can work in your and your teenager's favour at times. Good times and moments of pleasurable connection can be experienced with intensity too!

Some notes on other behaviours

When considering how to manage the behaviours outlined in Chapter Two, it is essential to remember that understanding the emotional need driving the behaviour is important (if we can address the emotional need we can influence the behaviour). It may be that other considerations are necessary too though in thinking about some of the challenges that young people can present with.

Lying and stealing

It is important to state at the beginning of this section that teenagers do lie; actually we all lie. As adults we tell children and young people that lying is wrong; I'm not going to argue that we should say that it is right, of course, but it is worth reflecting on the fact that people lie for a variety of different reasons without us judging all of these occasions as morally reprehensible or as indications that they will have serious problems with this in the long term. It is important for us as adults to be aware of our own relationship with honesty when we are addressing it with teenagers (they will certainly be more than ready to spot any hint of hypocrisy). The same principle applies to stealing. Young people may steal without it being an indicator of significant wider difficulties. It is considered normal for younger children to steal occasionally and this may pass as they progress developmentally; teenagers within this particular demographic may be delayed in developmental terms. Teenagers who have spent their younger years within environments where adults were dishonest may struggle with understanding appropriate behaviour.

When addressing these areas with young people it is important both to identify the potential reasons behind the behaviours and to frame the impact of these behaviours within the impact that they have on relationships. Many teenagers may not realize for example that lying and stealing affect trust and impact on parents' ability to feel safe.

I outlined a range of reasons as to why young people may lie or steal in Chapter Two. It isn't possible to go through all of the different possibilities here but I hope that some examples of addressing behaviours according to their underlying need will illustrate sufficiently the approach I am highlighting.

IF THE YOUNG PERSON DENIES ANY WRONGDOING BECAUSE OF A SENSE OF SHAME

Letting the teenager know that you understand why they find it so difficult to admit they have done something wrong, helping them to understand this and expressing empathy for their sense of shame are important. In doing these things you are helping them to understand their behaviour and expressing understanding of what is a very real difficulty. This allows for exploration of the possibility of the teenager doing things differently. Consequences do still have to be enforced but it is the 'figuring out together' of how he or she can change their behaviour that is most likely to effect change.

IF THE YOUNG PERSON IS CONSTRUCTING THEIR OWN HISTORY BY LYING

Again, it is important to recognize the emotional need within this behaviour. Accepting this need whilst explaining that the behaviour they are engaging in is unlikely to meet it provides the opportunity to think together about how to address this difficulty. The young person may simply find it too painful to think about the reality of their life and it is important to be accepting of this. You may think with them, though, about the downsides of not having a 'real' version of their own story (this is explored further in Chapter Six). You may suggest that you return to, or engage for the first time in, life-story work and be there to support them within this.

IF THE YOUNG PERSON LIES TO EVOKE NURTURE OR SYMPATHY

You can help the teenager to understand why they might be doing this – perhaps they find it too difficult to signal their attachment needs (attachment behaviour is explored further in Chapter Five) or perhaps their need 'isn't quite being met'. It may be helpful to support the young person to identify and explore the need they are really trying to meet so that they are able to receive more support for this. 'Upping' your nurturing behaviour may help the young person to feel that their need is being sufficiently met by you.

IF THE YOUNG PERSON STEALS BECAUSE THEY STRUGGLE TO FEEL SECURE

Some teenagers may take things such as food because they still carry insecurities about not having had enough to eat when they were very little. They may associate anxiety with hunger and/or still struggle to trust that the adults in their lives will meet their basic needs. As I have discussed in earlier chapters, these difficulties may rise to the fore again because the young person is aware that they are beginning to move towards independence. Helping the young person to identify these underlying emotional needs (and you may need to guess for them) and working out alternative strategies for managing this together are important. You may work out ways in which the young person can signal their anxieties more clearly so that you can offer reassurance or you may agree that they can have access to food in a way that helps them to feel more secure.

When we think back to the poor capacity that adopted teenagers have in regard to controlling impulses, weighing up risk realistically and understanding the impact of their actions on others' feelings (to take just a few examples) and combine these with the strong feelings that can drive stealing behaviours, it is possible to understand that the young person may have limited control over their behaviour. It may be necessary for parents to verbalize this awareness in their response to stealing and take practical measures to protect themselves until the young person is better able to change their behaviour. A parent might say, for example, that they know the young person just finds it too difficult not to steal and therefore the parent will need to keep valuables locked away until they have figured out how to support the young person in changing his or her behaviour.

Anxiety

In Chapter Two, Darren's anxiety and low self-esteem was an illustration of just how powerfully these feelings can impact on the young person's ability to manage daily life. It may be necessary to provide structures and support for the young person (as you would for a much younger child) in supporting them with these difficulties. Helping the young person to understand the link between their emotional struggles and behaviour is, as always, important in providing additional support. If anxiety and low self-esteem result in self-harming behaviours, it is important to seek professional support for these (this is discussed further in Chapter Four).

Sabotage

In Chapter Two, Darren's anxiety was at the source of his sabotaging behaviour. Other difficulties such as feeling that one is not worthy of positive experiences or an expectation that things will always go wrong may also influence sabotaging behaviour. If the parent is able to adapt their expectations of what the young person can manage because of these difficulties, it may prevent the repeated experience of 'failing' in planned activities or experiences. Again, identifying what the difficulty is, making sense of this and looking to whether it is possible to provide additional structures and support around helping the young person to manage is likely to be the most effective approach.

Managing controlling behaviours

I discussed the way in which positive experience of relationships can help to reduce the need for controlling behaviour in Chapter Five. Other strategies that may be helpful may be to provide high levels of predictability and consistency wherever possible within home life (and within the way in which you respond to the young person) and to allow the young person to have control over elements of their daily life wherever this is possible. Combining strategies that help to improve feelings of security whilst respecting the adolescents' need for some degree of autonomy and control in their lives are likely to be beneficial.

Drug and alcohol use

This is a tricky one, but I do believe that maintaining an open approach to discussing why people use drugs and alcohol, what the perceived benefits of these are and what the downsides may be is really important in helping young people make sense of their behaviour. Exploring with an open approach is more likely to be effective than simply saying 'Don't do it' if the young person is using drugs or alcohol. Being curious about what benefits the young person derives from drugs and alcohol helps them to make sense of what they are doing and is likely to keep the options for change more open. Sometimes the young person needs this input from professionals. Drug and alcohol teams are very knowledgeable and I have often found them to be useful in providing education for young people about the effects of alcohol and drug use as well as understanding the strategies that can be useful in reducing and (it is hoped) stopping harmful use.

Sleep

Chapter Two highlighted some of the contributory factors that can create difficulties for young people in this area if they have experienced earlier traumas and loss. Whilst there is lots of general advice available 'out there' about reducing arousal levels before sleep (limiting screen time and particularly gaming for example) addressing anxiety may be particularly important for adopted teenagers. It may be useful to use your relationship to reduce anxiety before bedtime (in the same way in which parents do for much younger children). Checking in with the teenager and using this time to talk through the day, for example, can help to reduce those anxieties that are related to a fear of being alone. Teenagers who struggle in this area may also need supports such as nightlights or a comforting snack before bedtime. A useful approach to thinking about what may be useful is to go back to how you managed any difficulties with sleep when they were much younger. Can any of these be adapted now? It may be helpful to reflect on these with the young person in helping them to make links and explore ideas of their own.

Boundaries and consequences for behaviour

The questions of which boundaries and consequences are appropriate, whether they are enforceable and whether they can be effective in adolescence understandably preoccupy many parents. There are very pragmatic reasons as to why enforcing boundaries and consequences can be significantly more difficult in teenage years: teenagers are much bigger physically (parents who may have picked up a toddler and said 'no' can't do this in teenage years); teenagers can 'vote with their feet' (they can walk away from their parents if they choose to); teenagers may not be impacted by punishments (they may choose, for example, to lose their pocket money if they decide that staying out at the party all night is worth it!). I find that it is useful to think in terms of punishment vs. consequences and rules vs. boundaries when I am negotiating this with young people and their parents.

Punishment vs. consequences

In *Helping Teenagers with Anger and Low Self Esteem*,[12] Sunderland argues that punishments on their own don't work in changing teenagers' behaviours because: they activate the brain's stress hormones and not the brain's pro-social systems; they make the negative relationship with the parent more negative; they often have a higher cost for the parent than the teenager; parents often can't stick to what they threaten; and constant criticizing and punishment means there is less space for the positive interaction (and the resulting feel-good chemicals) that is needed to keep the teenager's and parent's brains healthy.

Consequences that are a 'natural' consequence for unacceptable behaviour are likely to be a more effective approach than punishment in addressing behaviours. Examples of these may be: the young person steals and therefore loses that money from their pocket money in needing to pay it back; the young person punches a hole in the door and needs to pay for the cost of the breakage; the young person is rude to a family member and needs to make repair through an apology; or the young person steals from the local shop and has to go and make an apology and replace the value of the goods using any pocket money (or complete chores to earn the money to pay it back). Finding appropriate and enforceable consequences for behaviour is not easy (for example, in taking a mobile phone away the parent could lose the only way they can keep track of the young person and also compromise their safety). It can be difficult to find consequences that mean something to the young person, and they may chose to ignore them anyway, but the message of 'cause and effect' – that our actions carry consequences – is an important one throughout adolescence. The reality, after all, is that the outside world will certainly enforce consequences for poor behaviour. The reality of adolescence is that there is only so much control that the parent can exercise in regard to behaviour and for this reason it is even more important to keep the child invested in the relationship. This may not have immediate effects but it carries the best chance of influencing behaviour (aside from addressing underlying emotional needs) in the longer term. It is also important to remember to make sure that you are able to follow consequences through; it may be wise to wait until you are calm yourself in stating what a consequence will be!

Rules vs. boundaries

The message in enforcing 'rules' is that they are about parents' control. The message in providing boundaries is that they are about safety. Adolescents are more likely to respond to boundaries when they come with a clear message about the intention behind them and when they are collaborative, for example 'We are agreeing that you will come home at [X] time because it's safer to be using public transport before midnight.' Be clear about your own motivations for boundaries – where do they stem from, what is acceptable to you and why? Being clear yourself will make it much easier to communicate the reasoning to the young person. Clear expectations that are consistent without being rigid are also containing for adolescents, particularly those young people who struggle with difficulties in trusting parents to meet their needs.

Rewarding positive behaviour

Another strategy in influencing behaviour can be to focus on a positive factor to promote rather than inhibiting an impulse. This gives the young person an experience of being able to succeed and to have some control over their ability to make 'good choices'. Young people who are 'stuck' in negative behaviours can feel increasingly hopeless about their ability to have a positive effect on themselves and others. Finding even the smallest opportunities for young people to succeed in doing something vey well is very valuable. Even if these small successes seem trivial to us or irrelevant within the wider context of the young person's struggles, they are important to grasp. Any positive experience of the self is important in helping the young person (and often the parents) to hold on to the possibility that they are not the sum of their struggles.

Managing risk

Managing risk is likely to involve lots of practical considerations for parents, for example when to call the police if the young person is not returning home, hiding sharp objects if the young person self-harms or becomes aggressive, calling for professional support if the young person is using drugs, not providing money if they feel that the young person will use this for alcohol use or drugs and so on.

There may be other useful ways to think about risk that address some of the developmental and emotional needs. Developmentally, teenagers may need additional attention to thinking through the decisions they are making because of their tendency for hyper-rational thinking, their poor grasp of cause and effect and their difficulties in moderating impulses. It really is a learning process during this stage of development and although teenagers may resent the intervention of the 'adult brain', they really do need it! Reflection and working through decisions and sequences of events need to happen when the young person is calm but they are important in developing the young person's capacity for more 'top-down' decision making. This capacity does develop naturally as the young person moves towards later adolescence, and it can be reassuring to bear this in mind. Risk taking in mid adolescence tends to be at its peak; it reduces as the teenager's brain becomes more integrated in later adolescence. In later adolescence teenagers develop gist thinking (the capacity to draw on gut instinct and the knowledge/understanding gained from earlier experience). Supporting this integration through reflection and ongoing discussion may not bring immediate results when the young person is 14, but it will support that integration process.

Another approach that may be useful in managing risk is to provide safer experiences of taking risks for the young person. Fulfilling the need for that dopamine hit through high-adrenaline sports or taking part in challenges within organized activities may be a safer alternative to the need for adventure and exploration.

Conclusion

Whilst I'm sure that I haven't managed to address every theme, behaviour and question that parents have in this area, I hope that this has provided a useful starting point in beginning to think through some of the approaches and ideas that they may find useful. Other ideas and approaches in relation to specific themes are discussed in subsequent chapters. I will conclude here with comments and advice from parents on managing the emotional rollercoaster!

On the parent's influence

It's important to remember that there is only so much you can control – it doesn't mean that you aren't a 'good enough' parent if your child struggles. You may need to try lots of different ways of getting through to them.

Try not to go into 'This is something I've done wrong,' this is about much more than just your influence.

Don't feel that you are failing because your child is struggling; self-doubt and guilt is an easy spiral to get into. Sometimes you need other people to remind you of what you are, of how hard you are trying and what you are getting right. Hold on to those messages wherever you can get them!

On the particular challenges for adopted teenagers

Don't listen to those who say 'It's just teenagers,' or 'My teenager is like that,' if you feel that it is something more then trust your instinct and knowledge of your child. Talking to other adoptive parents can really help in validating your experiences.

On taking care of the parenting brain

When things get very stressed I leave the scene temporarily, just to get some space to breathe and calm down.

Don't feel guilty about having some time away doing something nice if you can, it will help your resilience the rest of the time.

On promoting the positive

Praise the positives, no matter how small. A post-it note under the pillow or on the fridge with positive messages can really help.

On maintaining clear boundaries

Having my own line on boundaries, even if they won't necessarily be followed, is important to me. I am clear about what I expect and why it is important to me.

On having realistic expectations

I have to be realistic about what he can do and I have to remind myself that he is emotionally immature.

On adopting a PACE approach

I found it helped to talk with her about what she thought was happening with the emotional swings, whether she was worried about it, if she thought there was a pattern and whether there was anything I could do to help. I tried to 'do a Dan Hughes' (the PACE approach) when we were both calmer. I think it did help.

On maintaining the relationship

Try and hold on to the good times and memories, think of them as 'something in the bank' for when things feel rough emotionally. If you can't, ask family/friends to do it for you.

Listening to someone else have a positive experience of my child gave me hope in regard to who he could be outside of the intensity of our relationship. A glimmer of who he might be post these tumultuous years.

On reflecting on your own teenage years and having realistic expectations

I found it helpful to talk with other parents about what I was like as a teenager. It's easy to forget those moments of rebellion that my parents never knew about, the sneaky cigarettes, underage drinking in my case... It helps to place what they are doing in a bit more of a context.

Chapter Four

MENTAL HEALTH PROVISION FOR ADOPTED ADOLESCENTS

In the preceding chapters I discussed some of the complex emotional challenges that can be present for adopted adolescents during this developmental stage and the varying impact of these on behaviours. This chapter will discuss the importance of adoption-focused provision for those young people who need additional support from therapeutic services within the mental health sector.

Dr. Ben Gurney Smith, consultant clinical psychologist at Adoptionplus, discusses important considerations for services and adoptive parents in navigating mental health provision as well as outlining considerations for effective support. I have provided examples of the experiences of young people and their parents which are inserted to highlight Dr. Ben Gurney-Smith's key points. I also provide the conclusion to this chapter.

The experiences of young people and their parents are highlighted throughout the chapter.

Mad, bad or sad: how services for mental health have developed

Whilst research has identified the profound and deep effect of interpersonal trauma and loss on young people's development, there has been an inevitable lag between this research informing practice and the commissioning and configuration of services to assess and address mental health needs in adoption. If one were to seek a shorthand for this state of affairs, and its lasting legacy for adoptive families, one might think of services organized around conceptualizations of difficulties as having origins that were either 'mad, bad or sad'. Understanding this history may help parents and young people when seeking or receiving services.

Traditional psychiatric services such as child and adolescent mental health services (CAMHS) sought to diagnose illness (i.e. the identification of 'madness') within the individual child to determine whether mental illness was present and therefore could be treated. Whilst this approach sought to recognize the increased rates of mental illness or diagnosable disorder in such a vulnerable population that 'looked-after' children undoubtedly were, many children still did not meet such criteria, particularly those with behaviour difficulties that masked underlying problems with emotional wellbeing and were difficult to assess in the face of oppositional or aggressive behaviour. Instead, their behaviour may have seen them enter the fringes of the criminal justice system and being known to forensic or youth offending services (i.e. seen as 'bad'). The disproportionately higher numbers of inmates with care histories confirms this. With the recognition of the developmental outcomes of maltreatment and loss (i.e. 'sad') particularly in the areas of emotional regulation (a cornerstone of mental wellness, and of attachment, associated with resilience and wellbeing), the impetus for the development of specialist services for looked-after and adopted children became apparent. By adopting a developmental approach, children and their families who might otherwise fall between the labels 'bad' or 'mad' could be both understood and helped.

For many adoptive families who find themselves struggling with the lasting effects of developmental disaster in their homes, however, this change may not be noticeable. Whilst services that adhere to a developmental approach do exist, which serve adoptive families well, their availability and accessibility is varied across the country. And for those families who receive services as usual that apply the 'mad' or 'bad' conceptualizations, they can either inadvertently feel they are the source of the problem or that they are advocating on behalf of all adoptive families who feel equally misunderstood.

> We have continually had to battle to get her what she should be entitled to. The post-adoption service claim they don't have the resources to provide specialist provision, mental health provision is scarce, CAMH services are often not 'adoption-aware' and residential support is even scarcer. Before you even begin to fight for all that you struggle to find a coherent and thorough assessment of what you should even be fighting for! Along the way you encounter suspicion and questioning of your own parenting, what you have 'done' for your child to be in such a mess.

This chapter focuses on the moment-to-moment impact of these conceptualizations as felt by families and outlines how to take an informed approach to understanding mental health services in adolescence and when and how to seek appropriate services to avoid disengagement for parents and young people.

> Oh my god, no way, if I have to sit there in a room while some crusty sits staring at me asking me how I feel or asking what I want to talk about I'll flip out man. You know, what is wrong with those people, how is that going to help? Can't I just have someone who will talk to me normally, not sit staring at me, I

just want to walk out of those rooms. Actually, scratch that, I will just walk out of the room, no 'want to' about it!

Now you see me, now you don't

Without any genetic link between a parent and child, services that do not take a developmental view of the difficulties sitting in front of them in the clinic room will lack an appreciation of the mutual influence of the parent on the child and of the child on the parent. New theoretical understanding underpinned by research now recognizes the impact of living with a child who struggles to trust the parent and of the parent's stress on the child's development. Anecdotally, this is often reflected in parents losing the original hopes and dreams they set out with in adopting, which 'at the end of the road' can look like critical and negative beliefs about the child.

It is imperative that a fuller and informed assessment takes the 'long view' by engaging families through understanding their original intent in becoming adoptive parents and what has changed.

> They were viewing us as these stressed out, incompetent parents who'd pretty much lost control of the situation. We are stressed and although we are struggling to manage I'd challenge anyone to manage in our circumstances. We are certainly not incompetent. I'm not sure that they really comprehended the journey we'd been on to get to this stage. We were in a good place 12 years ago (when we were approved to be adoptive parents). I still believe that we are very able to be competent parents; this has not been a 'normal' parenting experience. I'm not really sure that they could accurately understand our family without understanding that this is not how we started out as parents.

By doing so, much more informed assessment is possible about the nature of the problem too. Without this, parents can feel judged and further criticized in addition to their own internal negative dialogue, which often centres on a sense of failure as a parent. Furthermore, parents can find themselves removed from the process should they present in this way, when they are needed the most.

> The psychotherapist implied that I was controlling because I asked if I could be involved with some of the sessions or have regular feedback about the content. The implication was that I was part of the problem and not possibly part of the solution. I agree that he needs to have his own space, I know he needs it, I'm sure he probably wants to let off steam about us sometimes but this is a child who self-harmed after a letter from his birth mum, he cannot/will not talk about those early years (in his birth family) but I know that it's fermenting away in there. Isn't it possible that I could help him with that if I had advice? Outside of those one-hour-a-week sessions at least? We are there 24 hours a day 7 days a week. How do we talk about this stuff, how can I be helped to understand him if I'm excluded from all that?

Informed services will see the route to long-term recovery in securing greater openness of the parent and child to one another in attachment terms, particularly as the young person moves into adulthood and the process of negotiating new relationships with parents when they leave home.

Independence day

The autonomy and individuation that characterize the process of adolescence are likely to present differently in adolescents who have emotional regulation and attachment disturbance. Novelty seeking, including experimentation with alcohol and drugs, when emotional regulation is underdeveloped can lead to greater extremes of behaviour and with it the risk of mental disorder from substances. Without a sense of safety and security from attachment figures, these risks are accentuated. A recognition by professionals of the additional challenges this will pose to parents when seeking to address problems will be helpful. For example, discussing curfews with parents will be better informed if the professional understands that coming back home may not feel like a place of safety in the way a secure adolescent might.

Furthermore, an understanding that the chronological age of a young person may differ from the young person's emotional developmental age – that is the ability to manage stress and emotions and their levels of dependence on others to manage day-to-day tasks – will also inform knowing what level of independence is safe for a young person. It is also important to consider the young person's capacity to manage the therapeutic process and the way in which the service is provided within the context of the reality of their emotional developmental age.

> What was striking was the fact that some of the parents felt and indeed were excluded from the therapy, with one parent reporting that she had been told that her 13-year-old son should make his own way to the therapy (involving a bus and a tube journey). I felt quite unsettled by this, i.e. that a 13-year-old who is troubled by his early abuse, has an insecure attachment to his adoptive mum and may well find what comes up for him in therapy upsetting/unsettling is expected to journey alone and that his adoptive mum is excluded from the service and receives no advice/support in her role as a parent.

Dual diagnosis: all can have prizes

Without a formal psychiatric diagnosis, families may find themselves falling short of service criteria, which can only treat and intervene with a medical diagnosis. As yet, there are insufficient diagnostic categories to capture the varied symptom profile adopted young people can present with. Take these examples. Whilst post-traumatic stress disorder may match some of the symptoms young people experience, it lends itself better to one-off, discrete, life-threatening events, which is often at odds with the histories of multiple trauma of this kind in young people with a history in care. Furthermore, whilst problems with emotional regulation are recognized as symptoms of emotional disturbance, without other features being present either relating to attention, hyperactivity and concentration, or those often relating to an 'emergent personality disorder', they are unlikely to fit easily into psychiatric categories. The developmental effects on children's social development also pose diagnostic dilemmas with children presenting with autistic-type traits yet showing other signs that contraindicate this such as a developing capacity to make eye contact and form close confiding relationships. In these scenarios, families may find themselves 'bounced' between either an attachment perspective or that of a mental health approach when in practice both are equally possible and one need not exclude the other. Diagnosis is also hampered by limitations on the sources of information available that are crucial to making these developmental diagnoses, such as observational information of the child's social development in infancy and early childhood.

> My son was diagnosed as having autistic spectrum disorder (ASD) (Asperger's) at fourteen-and-a-half. Maybe not so unusual but I had been speaking to professionals and seeking help from aged six and had raised Asperger's as a possibility all that time. They said he had an attachment disorder and not Asperger's. At that time attachment disorder was fairly new to adoption and I now think not enough thought and assessment time went into his diagnosis. No one 'held' his case and no one followed through on what was happening. I kept raising the possibility of an ASD until finally I went

to the GP and asked for him to be assessed as his behaviour was becoming extreme (shouting at people in public and having serious meltdowns at home). I was also concerned, as the changes you would expect to see for children with attachment disorders, no matter how slow and painful, were not happening. Thankfully he was assessed and he is finally getting some targeted support. I think all adopted children should get a full assessment at the right age and parents should be supported to get the right assessments and help in dealing with the multitude problems our children face.

The mismatch between adoption-aware services perhaps found within adoption support and those applying a medical model can leave families falling between services in a seemingly semantic battle to describe the needs of the family to secure services.

The consultant claimed that B was not mentally ill, rather she had behavioural problems caused by being an adopted child whilst the post-adoption team claimed her problems were not related to adoption but were mental health problems. The family were caught up in the middle of this pissing contest between two teams of professionals.

It is possible to have a developmental or mental health disorder *and* an insecurity of attachment, which contribute to a detailed understanding of each individual young person. New research is looking at how maltreatment may impact on the child's capacity for relationships at a deep neurobiological level, which may lead to children 'looking autistic', and offers the prospect of greater clarity for young people and families.

Another way

Models of good practice in services that are adoption-aware and informed are likely to be marked out by the following features.

- Holistic: services that have qualified staff who have both an understanding and practice of mental health and adoption are likely to take a broad view and see that all aspects of the child's life as being relevant. These services will know when mental health services are needed as part of a care plan.

- Measurement services: these use multiple sources of measurement including structured interview, observation and questionnaire data across a range of domains of the child's functioning and wellbeing including their psychological wellbeing, attachment relationships, cognition, attention, memory and motor development to provide a fuller picture of the needs of the child and family. This will also include an understanding of where stress arises for the parent and child, the origin of this and the impact on the relationships within the family. Measuring change is also important when working with difficulties, which if developmental in origin, will have a longer recovery curve than acute problems and so good measurement can be repeated and inform both the family and the professionals on what interventions are needed over time.

- Multiple methods of therapy, which involve parents: the evidence base for therapies that improve the skills and understanding of parents is developing. Attachment-focused therapies such as Dyadic Developmental Psychotherapy are currently promising and match the presenting needs of young people and their parents in the difficulties in being parented and feeling they deserve love and care. Approaches such as these, which help improve the relationship, are likely to reflect a greater understanding and can be used to complement other approaches such as individual treatments for particular conditions. However, all should involve collaboration between all members of the family and team in an open and goal-orientated way.

I am so grateful for the services who have been able to work flexibly with my children and to meet their needs. They don't fit neatly into boxes and need more sessions than a standard six weeks of CBT [cognitive behavioural therapy]. Neither can they cope with psychotherapy by themselves and [they] need me to be there at least part of the time.

* Preventative: by identifying the needs soon after placement of the young person we can help prevent the development of what is often a core feature of families who come to struggle: stress. The day-to-day impact of living with a child who has learnt to be mistrustful should not be underestimated. This involves keeping a close and explicit watch for the parent and the child on the likely reasons for this. Services that can take a 'stay-healthy' approach to adoption rather than one that is reactive to difficulties are likely to keep shame and stress lower and secure support and services for the child and family in a pre-emptive manner, avoiding the harm of increasingly factious relationships. Regular health checks are likely to be part of this process so even when all appears well, the family knows that just as there is a need for a dental check, the family also needs a 'check up' too. This can facilitate engagement with services, particularly for children throughout their development.

When to be concerned about mental illness and to seek help

Knowing when a referral for a mental health assessment is required can be daunting. The following are pointers, which may aid decision making in discussion with a primary care health professional such as a GP.

- Have there been changes in the young person's sleep and appetite? Biological markers such as these may give an indication of possible illness.

- What impact are the difficulties having and where do they occur? If difficulties are happening at home and at school, there may be an underlying difficulty that needs a mental health assessment. Problems in just one setting may point to situational difficulties for the child rather than mental health difficulties per se.

- Positive and negative symptoms: so-called positive symptoms include thought disturbance such as holding unusual or odd beliefs, and hallucinations of any kind (visual or auditory) should be reported. Fears that are persistent, not open to reassurance and limit the young person's life are also relevant. Alongside this, negative symptoms characterized by the absence of functioning would include social withdrawal, loss of interests and pleasure. Both are a potential sign of mental health problems.

- Violence: where young people are involved in hurting others, it is important to seek help and this includes when the difficulties are at home with parents or young people are hurting one another. Often parents may try and understand their child's behaviour but this should not outweigh their own and their child's safety.

- Self-harm may reflect both difficulties regulating emotion and seeking comfort and care from others, but it can also signal conditions such as depression and body image distortion. If self-harm is present, it need not reflect suicidal intent, but can be risky and dangerous in its own right and so should be mentioned when considering a referral.

How to manage the maze of services on offer

The following may be helpful when thinking about what services are needed for your family.

- Ask for staff who are trained in the field of maltreatment or who provide services for looked-after and adopted children.

- Ask for services that actively involve parents in the treatment approach and emphasize relationships as being important to helping children in their recovery.

The following may be helpful when being seen by mental health services, so ensure you tell them:

- about the journey you have been on, what you hoped for and what has emerged now for you as a parent

- about what you know about your child's mental health history in their biological family taking any relevant documentation such as their medical documentation prior to adoption

- about what you know about how they managed and behaved in foster care or any previous care arrangements before coming into your family

- to look at the young person in their relationships with you (how easy they are to be comforted and cared for) as well as the need to see the young person in their own right.

Conclusion

Dr. Ben Gurney Smith's considerations for effective provision and the experiences of the adoptive parents commenting on their experiences of mental health services reflect many of the findings detailed in Julie Selwyn's report, which highlights many of the challenges that can exist in accessing effective mental health support but also the real value of good mental health support when this is available.[1]

> There were many complaints about mental health services for adopted young people. Parents described similar problems to those they had experienced with Children's Services. Parents complained about being unable to access CAMHS because of two year waiting lists; the child's difficulties were too complex for the service; there were no therapeutic services for children with attachment difficulties, and only being offered medication. In five cases, children refused to go for counseling.[2]

> Lack of expertise in working with sexual abuse, developmental trauma and attachment related difficulties were very apparent in the descriptions that parents gave of their attempts to get appropriate help from local CAMHS.[3]

Parents and young people do, of course, have very positive experiences of CAMH services. The difficulty is that these are inconsistent and parents are usually entirely dependent upon local variations, which may or may not be appropriate for their needs. Even for those parents who may receive additional funding for the specialist services (such as those provided by agencies like Adoptionplus, Family Futures, The Post-adoption Centre, Chrysalis and Catchpoint), access to those services can involve long journeys outside of their local areas.

My experience of local authority adoption teams is that they can also hold a great deal of confusion as to 'who provides what' in regard to therapeutic provision. This is often despite the fact that post-adoption teams have moved on significantly in regard to their understanding of the kind of therapeutic support that most suits the family's particular needs. Directing parents towards appropriate provision can be complex and confusing for even the professionals involved in children's services.

The availability of appropriate CAMH services for looked after and adopted children provoked the most concern. While LA [local authority] adoption services had become more therapeutic in response to the needs of adoptive families, managers stated that some local CAMHS did not have any clinicians who were trained in helping children with attachment difficulties. Managers mentioned that in some areas of the country CAMHS would not accept referrals from children with insecure attachments stating that there was no evidence base for interventions. Other CAHMS refused to acknowledge developmental trauma.[4]

Local authority post-adoption teams do have an important role to play in providing information and supporting referrals to mental health services for adoptive families. Knowing what the local CAMH services provide, the eligibility criteria, the length of waiting lists, the extent of provision, the nature of the therapeutic approach, whether provision includes parent support and so on is really important if children's services are to help adoptive parents navigate their way to appropriate provision.

Having systemic and informed referral processes to the therapeutic services available would be of huge value for adoptive families. Integrated and structured referral pathways, with readily available advice and information for adoptive parents, would ensure that parents were aware of referral processes, services available and the kind of information they need to prepare in order to fully inform mental health services of the difficulties they are experiencing.

Local authority teams should be empowered to argue for alternative provision if local services don't meet the needs of adoptive families. Mental health provision has long been the poor relation of health services and funding restrictions are a reality. The consequence of families not receiving sufficient support however can result in family breakdown and the young person entering the care system and becoming looked after. The financial costs of this outcome often far outweigh those that would have been required to meet the family's therapeutic needs.

Conclusion

I would like to conclude this chapter with further views and observations from the parents' perspective.

The statements above reflect parents' experiences and observations of accessing and receiving mental health services. Parents highlight the value of having an informed assessment in arguing for resources but also highlight the value, for them, of having their experience validated.

> I just kept banging on and on and on. After a while I didn't care what they thought of me, I argued and argued for an assessment and that was the best thing I could have done because they couldn't ignore that then. It was there in black and white from the psychologist and I wasn't 'imagining it'. They had to accept that that was what she needed.

Also important for parents is the value in services recognizing that they do know their child and have a valuable contribution to make to the assessment process, planning for therapy provision and supporting the therapeutic provision.

> You've got to find the services that understand it... You know when they do because they actually listen to you like you actually know your child (who'd have thought eh!). You

need someone who understands that there's another family present in this situation. They might not be physically present anymore but they are very much present for her. Her battles with us aren't just with us like they are for other teenagers. They are with them too and it's all mixed in together, if one more person tells me that all teenagers are like that(!). If only she only had that battle. I have to remind myself of that too though you know otherwise I'd go under.

In providing advice to other parents in this area, parents I have worked with have identified the following factors as being important in recognizing the need for and accessing services. They are reflective of many of the points raised by Dr. Ben Gurney Smith.

- If you are worried, seek advice from an adoption-focused service. If you feel that concerns are being dismissed, seek advice from elsewhere. Find a specialist agency that can give you a free consultation if you can. Find someone who understands.

- Inform yourself. Attend training and read about developmental trauma. Speak to other adoptive parents who might be having the same experiences as you and have experience of services (adoptive parents identified both Adoption UK and POTATO [Parents of Traumatised Adopted Teens Organisation] as services they had found particularly useful).

- It can help to write it all down. Cover the history of the situation, what you know about your child's early experiences and how things have been since they have been with you. Make sure that you include the positives as well as concerns. List your concerns and try and explain why you think they are more than just the usual 'teenage troubles'. Writing it all down can help you to be clear about what you are saying because sometimes when you are trying to get it across to professionals it can get a bit jumbled, particularly if you get upset!

- If there is mental illness in the birth family history, try to get clear information about what this was. I went back to the team that placed him to get more information and they were helpful with this. I knew there had been some depression but when we explored it, it was probably an understandable response to the circumstances those family members had been in. [I would add here that when there is a birth family history of mental illness that may carry genetic risks it is important to know this. At the same time it is also important to have informed advice about this as there are factors such as good-quality parenting and environment that can reduce these risks. Sometimes an awareness of serious mental health issues in the birth family history can escalate fears about a young person's behaviour (for parents and the young person) to a degree that doesn't actually reflect the reality of the risk. It is possible to interpret emotional difficulties that are entirely appropriate within the context of the child's history and development as being indicators of serious mental illness. They may be, but it is important to try and retain an open mind until an assessment can be undertaken.]

- This might not be appropriate in all situations but I asked my son if he was worried about the way he was behaving and was surprised that he said yes! This was helpful because it gave a message that it wasn't just us parents being paranoid. He was worried too. It gave him a message that we were in it together too I think. When we actually began the therapy I was surprised at how much he articulated about his own fears.

I would like to end this conclusion with further views and observations from the teenagers' perspectives in accessing mental health services.

Young people have often expressed their reservations about and difficulties in getting to therapy sessions on their own when it is a process that they find difficult anyway. For some young people, they may find a less structured and traditional approach more accessible, particularly if the worker can go to them rather than the young person having to travel to a process that they are strongly inclined to avoid.

> I do feel better because of it, it was sort of therapy wasn't it? I understood more and I felt like you understood. They need to understand that it puts people off, the getting on the tube/bus whatever, going into a room, someone sitting nodding at you, I'm not being funny but of course I'm going to get off the bus, go and do something that makes me feel better. I mean, they are nice people but you've got to help me do this stuff people, it's not like it's easy is it?

It is important to recognize that young people also hold fears about 'being mad' when they don't understand their own behaviour. 'Normalizing' their struggles and resulting behaviours within an understanding of the effects of early loss and trauma can decrease these fears.

> Normal is all relative really isn't it? I'm not exactly normal but I'm normal considering. Ha, if people had been through what I've been through. I've got my shit together considering, don't you think? If people are going to think they can judge on me I'm just going to think yeah right, like you'd know anything. They haven't been where I've been though.

> I was scared I was mad. I sort of get the adoption thing a bit now. It's all a bit mad really isn't it, it really pisses me off. At least I'm not mad though.

Young people do need a balance that reflects their need for some autonomy, and it is important for this to be assessed (this will be discussed further in Chapter Nine), however young people have acknowledged the benefits of their parents being involved in the work. One of the benefits I have heard young people acknowledge is that of feeling that their experience within their current family dynamics is observed and understood, that the dynamics between them and their parents are understood and that their views are also validated.

> I suppose I come because you make them [parents] listen. Sometimes it's about them and not me. They listen to you, they don't hear it the same way if I say it.

Mental health services that are able to meet the complex needs of this group of young people really are so important if we are to support adoptive families effectively. Good therapeutic services are incredibly effective in preventing family breakdown and can make a significant difference to the quality of young people's lives not just in the present, but also in the future. There is a huge level of need for services for adopted teenagers and their families.

Chapter Five

CHANGING RELATIONSHIPS

The Challenge of Managing and Sustaining Relationships with the Adopted Adolescent

This chapter will explore why relationships within the family change during adolescence and the biological and psychological reasons why this is necessary. It will also explore the additional challenges for adoptive families within this area, examining the process of separation and individuation from a 'wobbly base'. Approaches and strategies in managing the separation and individuation process will also be explored.

The adolescent need to separate and the challenges for parents

Adolescents need to begin the process of separation from their parents. The young person is preparing to move towards independence and the formation of adult attachment relationships, outside of their childhood relationships, that will sustain and support them in their adult lives. In biological terms, adolescents need to move away from their gene pool otherwise they will never reproduce! The parent–child relationship during this stage of development must inevitably change. Whilst separation needs to occur, though, it should not be a complete separation. Adolescents still very much need their attachment relationships during this stage; as I discussed in earlier chapters, they are absolutely crucial for the young person's security and emotional wellbeing as they navigate this process.

> While there is a natural and necessary push toward independence from the adults who raised us, adolescents still benefit from relationships with adults. The healthy move to adulthood is towards interdependence, not complete 'do it yourself' isolation.[1]

The task of staying connected to the adolescent teenager whilst enabling him or her to individuate and separate can be a challenging one in any family. Parents will often need to manage conflicting feelings and needs during this stage of development. They will need to: respect the young person's need to increase their own independence whilst recognizing the ongoing need for dependence; allow the young person increasingly to explore the wider world whilst keeping him or her safe; set and maintain boundaries that the teenager will need to push against; and offer advice and support whilst accepting that the young person will need to learn from his or her own mistakes. All of these are delicate balances for any parent and can be very fear provoking. Parents can also struggle with feelings of loss and rejection as they experience the young person's need for them changing. These feelings may be further impacted by some of harsher elements of the way in which some adolescents may begin to separate from them. Young people are unlikely to individuate and separate if they do not go through a process of questioning the status quo, and this includes questioning and evaluating their parents. Parents may find themselves on the receiving end of some fairly harsh evaluations of their parenting, value systems and even who they are as individuals. Teenagers themselves can struggle to make sense of these feelings and experience a great deal of anxiety and distress in relation to their new feelings about their parents.

Adolescents' feelings about their parents do, however, fluctuate. Whilst they may display critical and rejecting behaviours, they also, at times, need to be nurtured and taken care of as they did when they were a much younger child: 'The individuation process does not happen in a steady forward motion. There are times when the adolescent retracts into a state of dependence and abandons his separating and individuating process.'[2]

These moments represent opportunities for connection and nurture and can enable the parent to 'reconnect' in their parenting with their teenager. Responding to these needs can be tough when a parent is still reeling from the young person's more rejecting and critical behaviours. Being able to do so, though, is crucial in maintaining the attachment relationship.

Attachment and adopted adolescents

So, the challenge in managing changing relationships is clear even for those following the 'usual' developmental path of separation and individuation in adolescence. This process can be even trickier for those adopted teenagers whose early attachment relationships were impacted by poor parenting experiences. Four important factors that contribute to the additional challenges for adoptive families in this area are: many adopted teenagers are reaching this developmental process having had significantly less time with their adoptive parents (than other young people who have remained with their primary attachment figures since birth); many adopted teenagers will be affected by the more complex attachment history they have experienced because of their early lives; many adopted teenagers will be struggling with emotional immaturity; and adopted adolescents (like all adolescents) are at a stage of further identity formation, re-evaluating who they are and where they have come from. The adopted adolescent's identity formation is, of course, more complex because they are adopted. Identity formation is discussed in Chapter Six.

Adopted teenagers are often at a disadvantage developmentally because they were some distance 'behind the starting line' in developing their attachment relationships with their parents. Many adopted young people, for example, will only have had a limited amount of time with their adoptive parents before they entered into adolescence. Young people who were adopted at five or six years old will have spent approximately the same amount of time within the 'secure attachment promoting' relationships of their adoptive families as they did in the 'insecure attachment promoting' relationships of their birth families. Some children will have had to adapt to temporary attachments with other carers in between these two contrasting experiences. Whilst one would hope that the care received in foster placements would have represented healthier and more secure parenting styles, my experience is that this isn't always the case. Young people who have had less than sensitive and attuned care within foster placements will have experienced an additional layer of adverse attachment experience. Even when foster care is positive, these fleeting experiences of security will then have been felt as further losses and have required further adaptations. Even those young people who were adopted at a younger age will have 'lost time' in their attachment history, starting some way behind children born to secure birth families within which they have remained since birth. These young people, too, have missed out on the critical first year of being loved unconditionally without yet having to experience discipline and conditions on their behaviour. Adoptive parents can really struggle to help their children develop trust in them because they have missed this important stage.

Complex attachment histories can create additional challenges for young people's ability to use their attachment relationships during this stage of development. The introduction chapter provided an overview of the process of attachment in early years and discussed the nature of insecure attachments and internal working models developing in response to the caregiving experienced by the child who has suffered trauma and neglect. The fact that children's initial internal working models remain present even when healthier models have developed in response to good, attuned emotional care in adoptive families was also discussed. Many adoptive parents do experience significant changes in their child's ability to use their attachment relationships with them as they progress through their childhood. The consistent, attuned and sensitive parenting provided by the parents enables the child to use them for emotional support effectively, to feel more secure and to make improvements in their emotional regulation.

In adolescence, adoptive parents may begin to worry that the ground gained in attachment terms has been lost. Parents may begin to observe that their child struggles to use their relationship with them for support and nurture, shows increased levels of anxiety in being both separate and together or withdraws from the relationship to a degree that the parents feel unable 'to reach' their child. Many parents will feel that their child is 'reverting back to' the attachment style and behaviour they presented with in the initial stages of their placement with the family.

It is the case that earlier, more insecure attachment models can rise to the fore because this is a time of such huge change and transition for the young person. It is a time that inevitably raises stress and anxiety levels. As human beings we may revert to our more insecure attachment strategies (if these are our early formed models of attachment) when we are trying to manage high levels of stress. This is particularly the case when the stresses are attachment based.

Many parents express their feelings of sadness and empathy for their son or daughter in this particular struggle, recognizing that it presents a challenging conundrum. Their child has to begin to separate from the very attachment relationships they are reliant upon in order to manage their anxieties and fears effectively during a time when these feelings are increased! Moreover, they are further impeded in using these relationships effectively because of the move into more insecure attachment behaviours. In *Nurturing Attachments*, Golding writes that:

> [t]he transition to increased autonomy and reduced reliance on parents is a stressful one requiring the support of parents for its successful completion. Thus autonomy is most easily established from a base of secure relationships that will endure beyond adolescence. Adolescents can explore living independently from parents because they know that they can turn to their parents when they need to. Insecure attachment relationships lead to difficulties as the young person attempts to re-negotiate a relationship with parents. This can lead to a high activation of the attachment system at the same time as the young person is attempting to become more independent of parents.[3]

In the next section I will explore how more insecure attachment styles may be experienced and the challenges these can present for young people and their parents.

Additional challenges resulting from the 'wobbly base'

What impact does this separation process have when young people have continued to struggle with attachment relationships or indeed if earlier insecure attachment models are 'resurfacing' as a result of the stresses and anxieties of adolescence and changes in the teenage brain? It may be useful to think of the various challenges that can be present within the context of different insecure attachment styles. It is important to bear in mind that:

> As a baseline, we have one or some combination of the three 'organized' attachment models including security with its integrative functioning, avoidance with its overemphasis on the left-sided functioning and the minimization of attachment needs, and ambivalence with its right-sided development and the maximization of attachment needs. For some of us, terrifying experiences with our caregivers can result in disorganized attachment and the tendency to fragment our minds in dissociation.[4]

I will explore the organized insecure models of attachment (avoidant and ambivalent) and the way in which these can impact on adolescents as they move through the separation process below. The disorganized attachment style is also explored. Composite case studies highlight the way in which these styles may be experienced by the young person and his or her family and how therapeutic work can support families at this time. Approaches in working with the families in the case studies will also highlight the way in which the attachment styles impact on 'other ways of being' (according to the overemphasis of the right or left side of the brain) as well as behaviours within the attachment relationships.

The avoidant adolescent

Young people with an avoidant attachment style are recognizable in their tendency to be self-reliant; they find it difficult to seek support for emotional difficulties or to use their attachment relationship for nurture and soothing. Teenagers who have an avoidant attachment style are likely to value independence at the expense of relationships.[5]

In *Nurturing Attachments*, Golding highlights the 'expressed need' (the need communicated to others) of the avoidant child as one of needing to be left alone and get on with it.[6] The child fears closeness, as they have experienced their emotional need of the parents as leading to the parent's emotional withdrawal. When children need them most, the parents are least likely to be available to comfort and support. The fear of this loss of closeness and support is communicated as self-reliance, i.e. 'If I look like I don't need you then maybe you will stay close.' Paradoxically, the self-reliance of the avoidant child is the way they attempt to keep parents close. As the child grows older they become increasingly self-reliant, learning and taking pride in their ability to 'do without relationships' – the solution to fearing that others won't be available to meet their emotional needs and not to need others. These adolescents are likely to be focused on independence rather than interdependence. The impact on the way in which they begin to separate from their parents in adolescence may be to move too quickly and too far away from these relationships. 'Adolescents with an insecure-avoidant attachment pattern tend to direct themselves outward and leave their family prematurely... They have learned to withdraw when in trouble, or to fall back on their own resources.'[7]

When a young person has an insecure-avoidant attachment pattern, parents may interpret their separation behaviour as a 'normal' part of the adolescent need to separate and move towards more autonomy. It can be difficult to judge whether a young person's move towards independence is premature or not. However, if it feels to the parents that their teenager is moving too quickly towards independence, becoming too self-reliant and not using the parental relationship for any degree of comfort or support when experiencing difficulties, they may be recognizing that their young person is behaving in an avoidant way. Teenagers do need to use their parents' support in managing some of the many complex emotional challenges they will inevitably encounter. Without support to recognize or regulate these complex emotions, they are likely to emerge in unhelpful ways. Difficulties that may have been managed and alleviated with parent support can instead escalate. Whilst the avoidant adolescent may be giving parents a message of 'leave me alone, I'm fine' the reality is that they need support to accept nurture and to co-regulate (identify, meet and make sense of) their hidden emotional needs.[8]

Identifying and meeting these hidden emotional needs is a tricky balancing act for the parent, who needs to balance the separation process with the message of: 'You still need me, I am here for you.'

• • • • • • • • • • DANIEL AGED 15 • • • • • • • • • • •

In the first four years of his life Daniel had lived with his birth mother. She struggled with depression and was described by social workers as generally flat and unresponsive to Daniel's emotional needs. In the time leading to his removal from his birth mother, she and Daniel had been living in a homeless hostel. Staff at the hostel had expressed concern that Daniel was often found wandering around the building on his own. He had asked the staff for food and had been found rummaging through the bins looking for food. On one occasion, after Daniel had spent a considerable time playing in the staff office, staff members had realized that Daniel's mother had in fact left the hostel early that morning. Daniel had spent the day entirely on his own and did not seem distressed by his mother's absence. When reflecting on his early years Daniel told his adoptive parents that he remembered being in the hostel and was proud of his ability to look after himself at such a young age. He didn't seem to remember his time with his birth mother as particularly distressing. After his removal from his birth mother he had moved between foster carers twice in 18 months before being placed for adoption.

In earlier childhood Daniel had seemed to 'get along OK'. His parents reported few difficulties; he was an affectionate child who seemed to enjoy family life.

When Daniel entered adolescence his parents were initially impressed by the level of independence he demonstrated. Daniel seemed to have a busy social life, showed an impressive capacity to navigate his way around the city and was generally very self-sufficient. As time went by they did however begin to become increasingly concerned. Daniel's school contacted them to express concern about his behaviour. He was underperforming and had had a number of explosive altercations with his peers. One of these instances had involved Daniel attacking a pupil who had been making derogatory comments about a peer who was in foster care. Daniel was increasingly absent from the home. At weekends he had started to stay out all night and the parent of one of Daniel's close friends contacted his parents to let them know that there had been an incident when Daniel and his friend had been reprimanded by the police for what appeared to be antisocial behaviour. Daniel hadn't shared this with his parents.

Daniel was referred for therapeutic support but generally didn't make it to his appointments at the mental health team. A request was made for adoption-focused social work support in the hope that Daniel could be engaged in this way. The social work visits initially took place at Daniel's home. Daniel wasn't always in when he said he would be but did maintain contact by text message with the social worker and a relationship gradually began to build between them. Daniel would sometimes agree to meet the social worker wherever he may be and took advantage of the lifts offered to friends' homes or football practice. Daniel didn't share his parents' concerns about his behaviour, but it emerged that he had some motivation for engaging with the social worker when he asked if he would be able to have contact with a younger sibling (some seven years younger than Daniel) who had been removed from his mother's care. His younger sister had been placed separately for adoption but contact arrangements had never quite got off the ground. The social worker agreed to follow this up and, importantly, this provided a good opportunity for the social worker to engage Daniel in thinking about his early experiences with his birth mother. In wondering with Daniel about what sense he thought his sister might make of her removal from the birth mother, Daniel's assertions that his own experiences hadn't been too bad were gently challenged. The work was able to move into life-story work with Daniel and his parents as he began to show more curiosity about the reality of his experiences and the reality of the impact of them on him. As Daniel was increasingly able to reflect on what he had lacked from his birth mother and the sadness of his need for early self-reliance, he also began to make new sense of his relationship with his adoptive parents and his drive to be as self-reliant as possible in response to his focus on impending adulthood. Daniel's parents were supported to understand his behaviour as a part of his adaptive strategies to his early experiences and to understand that his 'emotional eruptions' were a signal of his unmet emotional needs. They were supported in proactively recognizing Daniel's attachment needs for him (as Daniel struggled to do this himself) and began to structure more 'together time' into their family routine. As Daniel progressed towards further therapeutic work he was beginning to access some of his painful feelings about his early life and it was anticipated that in using support to meet these as yet unmet needs his more worrying 'eruptions' in school and the community would begin to decrease.

The work with Daniel and his parents not only addressed his difficulties in using his attachment relationship with his parents but also aimed to begin to help him develop a more integrated brain. Siegel describes the avoidant brain as having an underdevelopment of the right hemisphere. Because it is this side of the brain that stores autobiographical memory and holds our raw emotional needs and feelings, this attachment style can mean that the adolescent will struggle with his or her awareness of their feelings and ability to make sense of them.[9] In supporting Daniel to reflect on and make sense of his early experiences, the work was directly addressing this imbalance and, it was hoped, moving Daniel towards a more integrated state.

The ambivalent adolescent

Young people with an ambivalent attachment style are recognizable in their intense expression of need of the attachment relationship. These young people will hold a fear that their attachment relationship may not be available. Teenagers with an ambivalent attachment style are likely to value (need) relationships at the expense of independence.[10]

In *Nurturing Attachments*, Golding highlights the 'expressed need' (the need communicated to others) of the ambivalent attachment style as one of needing reassurance of the availability of the parent. The young person expects the parent to be intermittently and unpredictably unavailable and therefore works hard to maintain the attention, literally to keep themselves in the parent's mind. They have an unconscious fear that they will be abandoned and forgotten without this effort. As the parent offers predictability and consistency, structure and routine, this need starts to reduce, but may increase again at adolescence when the developmental task is to separate from parents resurfacing old fears of abandonment.[11]

In *Brainstorm*, Siegel describes the ways in which this attachment style can leave young people with feelings of being alone or unseen. They experience a great deal of anxiety and uncertainty in regard to attachment relationships, fearing they won't work out. These young people often feel overwhelmed by interpersonal interactions; fear and anger mingle with the need for security and comfort.[12] 'Adolescents with an insecure-ambivalent attachment pattern oscillate between the desire for security in the family and the need to detach, needs they may have difficulty reconciling.'[13]

When a young person has an insecure-ambivalent attachment pattern, parents may find their separation behaviour confusing and overwhelming. The relationship may be filled with conflict whilst the teenager is, at the same time, expressing a high degree of need for the parent. These young people need reassurance that it is safe to be separate and to explore, even if this may feel scary. The parents need to provide reassurance that they remain available and consistent. The young person's hidden need[14] is for support to be apart.

• • • • • • • • • • • BECKY AGED 15 • • • • • • • • • •

Becky had been removed from her birth family because of concerns about her parents' neglect of her needs. Both of her parents were addicted to heroin and their lives were chaotic because of this. Becky's parents were not intentionally cruel and they could be very loving and attentive to Becky's needs. Unfortunately, as their drug use got more and more out of control, their care of Becky became more inconsistent. They were increasingly focused on their need for heroin, what they needed to do to get it and using it. Their attunement to Becky's needs decreased as their addiction escalated. They were more and more inconsistent in their availability to Becky. At times she experienced love and nurture; at others an 'absence of' her parents. Prior to Becky's removal at the age of three years, neighbours had called the police after they saw Becky leaning out of an upstairs window. Becky had been left at home alone. When police entered the family home they discovered a dirty, chaotic and cold environment. There was very little food in the home and although Becky's bedroom looked as though it had at one time been well furnished with toys available, it was clear that the home was in a serious state of neglect. Becky was cold, hungry and in a distressed state.

As Becky had grown up with her adoptive mothers, they had worked hard to increase her trust in their relationship. They both worked primarily from home and Becky had therefore experienced a high degree of availability from her mums. Both of her parents understood that her early experiences had left Becky with a fear of abandonment. They had been particularly careful to provide Becky with predictability and consistency, had provided a high level of nurture in their care and had supported Becky in increasing her confidence to manage within the school environment and being separate from them as she was gradually able to enjoy play dates at friends' houses and other activities outside of the home. They loved Becky dearly and were proud of the progress she had made.

When Becky was 14 years old her Scout group organized a camping trip by the coast. Becky was keen to go and her parents were glad that she was showing signs of wanting to have some degree of independence from them. The young people were allowed one phone call home a day whilst they were away and when Becky checked in with them she seemed to be OK. When the Scout group returned from their trip Becky's parents went to pick her up. When they collected her they were surprised that she seemed grumpy and cross with them. One of the Scout leaders took her mum aside and explained that they had struggled with Becky's behaviour over the previous two days. She had refused to go to sleep at night, talking to the other young people to the extent that they complained about not being able to sleep. She had been attention seeking and disruptive during the group exercises. This incident seemed to trigger a level of anxiety for Becky that continued after she returned home and for a considerable period of time afterwards. Although Becky continued with her previous activities and spent time with her friends, her parents worried that Becky was again feeling insecure in her relationship with them. She was often irritable with her parents when she returned home, struggled with her emotions and often accused them of not understanding her or of having let her down if there were any changes in routine and plans. Becky seemed distracted at school and was increasingly disruptive at home, not allowing her parents to work when she was at home and seeking any kind of attention even if it was negative. Becky's parents felt that they were caught up in a whirlwind; they hadn't changed in their approach to Becky and yet they felt that they couldn't give her enough to meet her needs.

Becky and her mothers were referred for adoption-focused therapeutic support and began dyadic developmental psychotherapy (DDP)-focused work. As the therapeutic sessions progressed, Becky was supported to understand the feelings underlying her behaviours. One of the things that emerged was that Becky had struggled to be away from her parents during her Scout trip. She had felt alone and anxious even though she had been surrounded by her peers during the trip. She had particularly struggled at night-times as others in her tent drifted off to sleep and she had been left alone, unable to sleep and feeling upset. She had felt frustrated by the limits of the phone calls home and described feeling that her parents 'didn't say enough' during the phone calls. On further exploration it became clear that these phone calls were not sufficient to help her feel connected enough to her parents. On the day that her parents had collected her, the Scout group had returned earlier than expected. Although her parents had been on time to collect her, she had waited half an hour before they arrived. Eventually, Becky was able to articulate her feeling that in this timeframe she had been convinced that her parents were not coming to pick her up, that they had 'changed their minds' and decided that they didn't want her anymore. This profound and painful feeling of abandonment had been overwhelming for Becky. Since that time she had experienced very conflictual and distressing feelings in relation to her sense of her parents' availability to her. Whilst she wanted to go out and spend time with her friends, this escalated her anxiety; as her behaviour became more difficult she became convinced that it was only a matter of time until her parents would 'return her' to foster care. She interpreted her parents' responses to her through this insecure lens. If they were working, it was because they didn't want to spend time with her; if they didn't respond quickly enough to her distress (or indeed notice her distress), then they didn't understand her or love her. It was exhausting for all of them. Becky's tentative approaches towards separation in her trip away and increased need to spend time with her peers had triggered her insecure-ambivalent attachment behaviour.

Becky needed support in understanding where her feelings of fear of abandonment and neglect belonged. She needed support in understanding that her overwhelming feelings of 'You are not there for me, you don't see me, you don't want me,' were feelings and not facts.[15] Life-story work helped Becky to reflect on and make sense of her early experiences of neglect and abandonment. Her parents were alongside her to feel her pain and sadness and to provide messages of support and reassurance about their own commitment to and love for her. They were clear that, had they been her parents, they would never have let her be left alone, frightened and abandoned. They were able to reflect on and anticipate the times when Becky may experience them as unavailable, to articulate this awareness for Becky when she felt lost in her feelings and to help her to reconnect with them. They were accepting that Becky's adolescence and need to separate was going to be challenging for her and that the pace of this process would need to be carefully balanced.

• •

Like Daniel, Becky needed additional support in making sense of her history and understanding the way in which her early experiences were impacting on her ability to use her attachment relationship with her parents. In contrast to Daniel though, her ambivalent brain had an excess of emotional right-sided activation. She was often flooded with feelings and implicit memories as she began the process of beginning to separate from her parents. The life-story work process (within the context of her wider therapeutic work) helped her to begin to become more integrated. She was able to use the linear, logical left brain in cooperation with the right brain (where autobiographical memory is stored) to develop a more coherent account of her history and gradually to become less overwhelmed by her fears.

The disorganized adolescent

Young people with a disorganized attachment style are recognizable in their unpredictability in response to managing stress. They are not able to rely on themselves or their parents in a consistent way. They are often highly controlling in their attempts to feel safe.[16] Teenagers with this attachment style are often in an extremely fearful state. They are the young people who experienced their early attachment figures as a source of terror. They remain immersed in unresolved trauma and loss. The past may be experienced as being in the present; their early trauma continues to be terrifying, confusing and intrusive. Adolescents with a disorganized attachment style are easily dysregulated and emotionally overwhelmed.

In *Nurturing Attachments*, Golding highlights the 'expressed need' (the need communicated to others) of the older disorganized child as one of needing to be in control.[17] These children do not feel safe with relationships and they seek to control others rather than enter into reciprocal relationships. Frightened of being influenced by others, they use control as a way of influencing without being open to influence. The hidden emotional need, though, is for help in feeling safe and to emotionally regulate. The controlling attachment style means, however, that they struggle to allow others to provide them with this. These young people are likely to act out their feelings rather than understanding or processing them. They are unable to think about or reflect on how they or others are feeling. They need a low-stress environment and support to trust others to help them to emotionally regulate and to help them develop their reflective functioning capacity. Managing and responding to the adolescent with the disorganized attachment style is extremely challenging. Parents need to try and provide a home environment that is as safe and supportive as possible, as the young person's attachment behaviours are likely to place a great deal of stress on relationships. The young person's need to move out towards the world and begin to separate will increase stress and risk as she or he struggles to manage her or his responses outside of the home.

• • • • • • • • • • AMBER AGED 13 • • • • • • • • • •

When Amber was removed from her birth family at the age of two she had a number of significant injuries. She had lived in a home characterized by domestic violence and had clearly been injured on a number of occasions by either one or both of her parents. Amber had struggled in her adoptive placement since the time she was placed with her adoptive mother at the age of three. Amber had been physically aggressive towards her mother from the early stages of placement. Although she would approach her mother for comfort at times, her responses to her mother's attempts to sooth her were 'jumbled' – she would bite her mother whilst being held in her arms and lash out as her mother tried to approach her. Amber was a hyper vigilant child; she responded to her peers with dominance and aggression despite desperately wanting friendship and was often distressed and confused as she experienced rejection from her classmates. When Amber began to move into adolescence her behaviour became more erratic. She began to run away from home and was at risk of being groomed by abusive peers and adults. She sought out peers who were also displaying risky behaviours and often formed intense friendships, which would then quickly deteriorate and descend into physical fights. Amber was demanding of her mother and tried to control her mother's actions but was unable to use the relationship to meet her emotional needs. Amber's aggression towards her mother increased and her mother was increasingly concerned about her own and Amber's physical safety.

The concerns about Amber's level of risk to both herself and others led to child protection procedures being instigated. The local authority recognized that the family required specialist therapeutic support, and funding was allocated to provide intensive support from a specialist adoption support agency.

The first steps undertaken in working with the family were to put in place a safety plan, both in regard to the violence that Amber was displaying at home and to her running away. Amber's mother was helped to draw up a plan of support and intervention using both her own support networks and the professional networks (including school and the police). Amber was made aware of these strategies and a clear message of the need to address both her safety and her mother's safety was communicated to her (information about facilitating these kinds of strategies is available in Chapters Three and Nine).

An intensive therapeutic plan was put into place alongside the practical strategies for managing risk. Support for Amber's mother was prioritized, as it was recognized that she needed significant support to manage the levels of stress that she had been experiencing for some time. Focus was given to the impact that Amber's difficulties had had on her mother's experience of being a parent; her own confidence in her own capacity to parent had been severely impeded. Amber's mother was also prepared to begin to take a 'therapeutic parenting stance' alongside exploration of the impact of Amber's early experiences on her early development and resulting attachment behaviour. As Amber began to join the therapy sessions (which were structured and focused in the same way as Daniel's and Becky's input) particular consideration was given to allowing her as much control as possible. In this way Amber was supported in feeling safe enough to engage with what would be challenging work for her. Theraplay techniques were also used to help Amber engage with her mother in a way that gently challenged her need for control.[18] As the work progressed, Amber was able to make gradual but significant progress in beginning to make sense of her history and her relationship with her adoptive mother and to begin to recognize her attachment needs and signal them more clearly. Work with Amber would need to be long term in nature – her difficulties were profound – but the crisis of adolescence had provided a trigger that had eventually provided the support that could lead to a more hopeful future for both Amber and her mother.

The work with Amber would be crucial in addressing the profound lack of integration in her developing brain. The disorganized adolescent experiences a 'fragmentation of the mind'. From the early stages of her placement Amber had been overwhelmed by implicit memories (stored in her mind before the age of two years) of a need for her attachment figure being met by physical pain and distress. Making sense of the events in her life that made no sense could potentially help her mind to become more coherent and help her to function in a more integrated manner. Helping the limbic region, the hippocampus, to integrate implicit memories into facts and autobiographical recollections could directly impact on her capacity to move towards a securer attachment style[19] and to be able to use her relationship with her mother to meet her emotional needs. The limbic region and hippocampus areas of the brain are significant because they are the key in integrating implicit memory into explicit memories of facts and autobiographical recollections. Further explanation and exploration of the functions of these parts of the brain can be found in Daniel Siegel's *Brainstorm*.[19]

Conclusion

Navigating the shifting sands of the changes in the relationship with the adopted adolescent will, inevitably, present challenges for parents. Previous chapters have discussed the huge impact of loss for adopted teenagers but I emphasize again that loss is also a significant theme for adoptive parents. Whilst this may be present for all parents of teenagers, it carries additional complexities for adoptive parents. The particular nature of their child's difficulties may make it feel as though the relationship is at risk of breaking down entirely. In order to understand what is happening within the relationship with the young person, parents will need to be attuned to the emotional needs underlying their young person's behaviour. This can require a 'counterintuitive approach', as young people are often unable to signal their attachment needs clearly and parents may well require professional support in helping their child. Parents need to be resilient and robust in responding to the adolescent's attachment needs and may need to be particularly attentive to their own attachment needs during this stage (refer to Chapters Three and Nine).

Despite the additional challenges, paying attention to the attachment relationship in the teenage years offers more opportunity for change and balance. It may seem like a rockier road, but not all is lost. Important work can be undertaken during this time that carries huge benefits for the young person. We must remember the particular plasticity of the brain during this period and the opportunity that the changes and challenges provide. Retaining a relationship despite the challenges is a message that change does not equal absolute loss, that many ruptures do not mean catastrophic breakdown and that relationships can change, adapt and be repaired (even after many, many ruptures!) and emerge even stronger. For the young person whose early life was characterized by trauma and profound loss, this is the most valuable message of all.

It is important to note that some young people will leave their adoptive families before they are 18. They may re-enter the care system, return to birth families, enter the criminal justice system or go to live with friends or boyfriends and girlfriends.

It is my experience that when this happens the vast majority of parents still try to maintain a relationship with their child. They still worry about the young person, still have their best interests at heart and still provide support to the young person even if they are no longer living at home. The parenting role does not end just because the young person is further away. It is unfortunately the case that services often don't appreciate or manage to support parents in their ongoing attempts to maintain a relationship with the young person. This could be because services may take a 'blaming stance' towards parents, viewing the family breakdown as being caused by faults in their parenting. It is also often the case, though, that services with scant resources are not able to provide the level of support that young people and their parents need if the young person leaves home. The value of maintaining the relationship, wherever this is possible, cannot be underestimated.

I would like to end this chapter by returning to parents' experiences of changing relationships in the adolescent years. The observations below include notes about parents' experiences and also strategies that they have found useful in maintaining positive relationships during this stage.

On reflecting on the 'wobbly base' of attachment

We tried to be a safe harbour as well as a launching pad but the balance between the two was very much complicated by the fact that he had always struggled with the 'safe harbour' bit!

On the uneven move towards separation

One minute she would be shouting and stomping up the stairs, then moments later would want to come and sit on my lap for a cuddle.

I'm looking at him sometimes thinking right, are you 5, 15 or 25 today? Are you going to ask for banana milkshake (his

5-year-old obsession), moan about GCSE coursework or announce that you are off to an 'all nighter' on Saturday? Which age parent do I need to be?

On finding the connection times

Whatever you do, try and find some way to maintain a connection when they let you. My daughter pretty much rejected everything except going to have our nails done together. I had very groomed nails for a while! It was at least a time when we could be side by side enjoying something without stress.

Seize on opportunities to be together when they do arise, sometimes I get more out of her in terms of a meaningful conversation when I'm giving her a lift somewhere. I resist the 'What am I a taxi driver?' line and think well maybe we'll get a chance to talk.

This is essential, finding the positives and a way to do something together so that they can come back in from the cold. Doesn't really matter what – going for a pizza, decorating a room, visiting a relative, going to a football match, shopping…

On keeping the lines of communication open

Texting can be a godsend as a less intense way of maintaining a link – particularly when they are out and being a bit non-responsive. I class getting a text message back as a major victory.

When she was staying away I used to text to say good morning and good night religiously. I wanted her to know I was still thinking of her, I wasn't asking questions that would require a response (that might annoy her!). It was hard but I was saying

'No pressure, don't freak out, I know you don't like me very much right now but I'm still here.'

Is the phone a transitional object? I don't know but when she was little I was advised to give her a photograph of us to take to school or a toy from home, a sort of 'Hey we still exist' message. I see her phone in that way a bit. I can leave messages 'I'm still here.' It's a bit like an extended umbilical cord.

I tell him that he's welcome to invite his friends round, I don't like some of them but it's a connection to his world that I can be a part of for those moments. I save all of their numbers to my contacts if he needs to call from their phone when he's run out of credit or lost his (again) then I can call them when I'm trying to track him down.

On focusing on what is going well in the relationship

I would say notice the parts of the relationship that are still alive and well, no matter how small. Tell them when you have enjoyed their company: 'Look our relationship is still here' even if it's changing.

I think that often parents probably need to change their expectations. Don't compare yourself to friends who have children who seem to be lovely, perfect, super balanced, still going shopping with their parents teenagers (can I say 'yuck'?). Compare like with like I say: talk to adoptive parents!!! You'll feel less inadequate.

On looking after yourself and using others for support

Use other relationships within the family if you can, they may like your child for you when you can't quite manage it! They can be useful in providing a different perspective of your child as well. My son can be his lovely charming self when he is with his uncle. It reminds me that that is still a part of him.

Use the relationships that make you feel good for your own sanity. The friends who will say 'You are not a crap parent' without trying to give you useless advice!

I wouldn't have got through this without the support of my husband, he picks me up when I am feeling a bit too bruised.

On coming out of the other side

Remember, this won't stay the same. Believe that it will get better.

I would say that she still has a high need of me, more so than my friend's children who are that age. She lives nearby but has been able to have own relationship and family. I'm proud of her.

He maintains contact now and suggests that we meet up, sometimes confides in his dad particularly. Not a 'close close' relationship and it's generally on his terms but a relationship nonetheless, I'd say that's a success, there was a time when I thought he was just going to decide that we were no longer relevant at all to him.

Chapter Six

EMERGING IDENTITY

Identity formation is one of the key developmental tasks for adolescents. This chapter will consider the universal nature of identity formation and its purpose, whilst focusing primarily on the relationship between adoption, early loss and trauma and the adolescent's emerging identity. I will explore the particular challenges that can arise for adopted young people in developing a healthy identity. The impact of these challenges on parents will be discussed and potential approaches and strategies for managing these challenges explored.

The importance of identity development in adolescence

When adults look back on their teenage years (and the photographic evidence of it) there is often much embarrassment and amusement at the 'phases' that the individual went through. Photographs often document a variety of experiments in fashion styles, passionate affiliations with certain musical styles, political affiliations and an interesting myriad of hairstyles. Whilst amusing, these 'phases' are often a physical representation of the important process that all adolescents must move through in forming an individual sense of identity as they move towards early adulthood.

Erikson's theory of identity development[1] describes this stage of development as one of identity vs. confusion. During this developmental stage young people are moving towards their individual adult identities. According to this theoretical perspective, if an adolescent receives encouragement and reinforcement during this stage of development, he or she will emerge with a strong sense of self and a feeling of independence and control. The emerging young adult will be able to live by society's standards and expectations with a reintegrated sense of self.

The quality of mind of 'creative exploration'[2] drives young people to understand their own stories in a new way. Brodinsky[3] describes the new phase of cognitive development in teenage years and the capacity for abstract thinking as allowing a teenager to focus on matters of morality, philosophy and esoteric questions such as 'What is the meaning of life?'. This new capacity can be experienced as hugely exciting, inspiring and novel for many adolescents as they begin to make sense of the world in which they live in a new way. At the same time, adolescents are experiencing a focus and questioning of 'self' with the capacity that this new stage of cognitive development allows. Moretti and Holland describe this process in the following way:

> The capacity of adolescents to simultaneously consider multiple perspectives in the self, in concert with rapid transition in their social roles and relationships provokes a period of intense self-preoccupation and pressure to consolidate a sense of self.[4]

The focus on self leads to the 'trying on' of different ways of being for adolescents (hence the photographs that provide an interesting visual record of this period). Identity is in a fluid state, a process that involves moving away from the parents' values as the adolescent forms a new individual identity. This process can be an intense, creative and vibrant part of teenage life. It can also, however, prove to be a very challenging process. Some teenagers will face additional struggles in forming a positive identity and sense of self depending on the degree of acceptance their developing identity receives from family, friends and wider society for example. Some will need to form a secure and positive sense of identity within a society that may well discriminate against them. Lesbian, gay, bisexual and transgender young people may face additional challenges in developing a positive identity within the context of cultural messages that are negative, as may adolescents from different religious, racial and cultural backgrounds. All teenagers will generally need to navigate cultural messages about gender and sexual identity that can be very confusing and challenging. It is a complex process and at no other stage in our development do we experience the intensity of this questioning and experimenting in relation to ourselves.

'Being adopted' and the fact that this will be different to peers who live in their birth families may in itself bring more complex feelings at this stage of development. Although teenagers often express a need to be different and unique they also often find 'being different' in their adoptive status very difficult. This is a difference that isn't of their choosing and carries far more complexities than choosing an identity within a range of 'acceptable' teenage alternative identity groupings. The diversity of family arrangements can also create some additional challenges for adopted teenagers as they begin the process of individuation. Young people who have grown up within transracial or transcultural adoptive families, with extended birth family members or with gay or lesbian parents may experience more complex and challenging feelings about this aspect of their identity as they move through this process.

Why this process may be more complex for adopted teenagers

Integrating birth and adoptive identity

Adopted teenagers may experience this process as being more complex than it is for their peers who have grown up in their biological families. The very nature of the process of questioning who we are, with whom we identify and who we are destined to be carries an additional layer of meaning for young people who are not growing up within their birth family. There is another genetic identity that the young person needs to make sense of and integrate into their identity formation.

For many of the young people I have worked with, their question in relation to their developing identity during this stage has at its simplest been: 'Am I like my birth family or am I like my adoptive family?' (and often, by implication: 'Where do I belong?'). The questioning of 'Who am I?' requires the young person to make sense of their experiences, navigate the 'nature vs. nurture' debate and individuate within the context of two (often starkly different) experiences of birth and adoptive families. When we consider the fact that this process can be a conflictual and unsettling process for those adolescents who only have to do this within the context of their only (birth) family, it is easy to understand why it can raise many additional challenges for adopted young people.

The nature vs. nurture debate is one that frequently arises within adoption; what makes us who we are? Our cultural references are filled with messages about the importance of genetic identity and the powerful influence that this has on our destinies. How many times have we heard phrases like 'The apple doesn't fall far from the tree,' and 'Blood is thicker than water'? In adolescence, these messages may take on a new meaning for the young person who has a new capacity for conceptual thinking. Young people who are physically changing and maturing may also begin to look much more like their birth parent(s). This can be unsettling for both the young person and their parents, as it can highlight physical differences between the young person and their adoptive parents and increase their curiosity about other aspects of themselves that they may share with their birth family.

When there are gaps in information about birth family identity

Many adopted young people who are in their teenage years today will have information about their birth families. Many will have life-story books and photographs of their birth families. Some will have had ongoing contact and updated photographs from their birth family throughout their childhoods (the potential benefits of this in relation to identity will be discussed in Chapter Eight).

Many young people, though, won't have information about their birth family. For some, an absence of information may be in relation to who their birth parents are. I have worked with a number of young people who have no information about who their birth father is for example. Some young people will experience this absence as a very painful one: 'I just want to know who he is.' Whilst this pain may be related to loss, it can also be related to the difficulty for the young person in trying to understand and make sense of who are they are. In the absence of information, some adopted adolescents will 'fill in the gaps' themselves with fantasies about this part of their genetic identity. Others may begin actively to search themselves in order to find the answers to their questions. Both of these strategies carry their own risks. Fantasies about birth parents may be either entirely negative or positive. Negative fantasies can impact on the young person's sense of their own identity and self-worth.

I used to think that they were really extreme, gangsters or something else really bad… I kind of thought yep that's me.

Because of when I was having problems with my anger and stuff.

Positive fantasies can cause difficulties for young people in creating a coherent narrative about their lives. If a young person was removed from their birth family because of serious concerns about their welfare, they need to have a realistic narrative about what happened and why. If the young person's fantasy is that their birth parents were simply misunderstood, this could compromise their safety, as they may initiate contact with a birth family member who could pose a risk to them. Alternatively, young people's denial that there were any difficulties with their birth parents could lead them to conclude that the difficulties must therefore have lain with themselves. This can be disastrous for their own sense of positive identity.

Making sense of the birth family identity when the young person's early experiences were harmful

Young people who are aware of their early history may be trying to understand: the nature of their birth families; why traumatic events happened to them because of their birth parent's care; and why their birth parents behaved in the way they did. Their understanding of who they are and who they will be within the context of this can be both confusing and frightening. Some adopted adolescents will 'try on' aspects of what they imagine to be their birth family identity as they try to resolve these questions:

> [I]n an effort to symbolically ditch his childhood identity, an adolescent may move in directions frightening to his parents. He may, in fact, choose to identify with elements he associates either with his fantasies or with the realities of his birth parents' lives.[5]

Unfortunately, some of these aspects of the birth family identity may be the kinds of behaviours that led to the young person being removed from the family and may include: experimentation with drugs and alcohol, chaotic and irresponsible behaviour (including criminal behaviour) and behaviours within relationships that are potentially harmful to the young person and others. These behaviours may be related to this identity process; they may of course also be present for the young person because of the developmental and emotional challenges they are facing (see Chapter Two). The question of whether the young person is 'choosing' to engage in behaviours as a part of identity exploration (this may not be a conscious choice) or whether the behaviours are present because of emotional and developmental challenges can get very muddled. Some young people may temporarily engage in these explorations but others may conclude that the behaviours they are struggling with are 'genetically predetermined'. Often there will be elements of both of these factors.

• • • • • • • • CHRISTOPHER AGED 14 • • • • • • • •

Christopher had experienced neglect and domestic violence within his birth family. He was eventually removed from their care and placed with foster carers before being adopted at five years of age. Christopher had experienced a high degree of fear on (probably) a daily basis for the first four years of his life. He had been a child in a constant state of hyper vigilance, waiting for the next overwhelmingly frightening incident to occur with very little available comfort or opportunity for soothing from his birth mother, who was unable to be attentive to his emotional needs. As a consequence, Christopher had continued to struggle throughout his childhood with emotional regulation. He was a child set on high alert to potential danger and often moved into angry outbursts as he struggled to contain his feelings. As Christopher moved into adolescence, these difficulties were amplified. The changes in his teenage brain combined with the vulnerabilities resulting from his early experiences resulted in even more rapid and frequent explosions of frustration and anger. He was a young man who perceived threat everywhere around him. His parents worried that Christopher took pleasure in his anger; he had often stated that he felt 'strong' in this moments. Christopher was aware that his birth father had been a violent man but had limited information about him. He had had letterbox contact with his birth mother throughout his childhood but not with his birth father (letterbox contact refers to the process of exchanging information between birth and adoptive families via Social Services. It is the most common form of post-adoption contact and is discussed further in Chapter Eight). Christopher had lots of questions about his birth father but the only 'concrete' information he had was that his father was a man who was feared within his local community because of his violence. Christopher wondered if his difficulties with anger meant that he simply 'took after' his father. In some ways this frightened him; he worried that he was destined to be a violent man with all the potential consequences that this may bring. He also, though, felt some connection to the birth father he felt such an 'absence of' in his anger. Although muddled and frightening, this reasoning fulfilled some need for certainty and fuelled his adolescent fascination with fantasies of predetermination and destiny.

Christopher's parents also expressed fear that his difficulties with anger were somehow genetically 'inherited'; they had been very aware of the fear held by the professionals in regard to his birth father at the time when Christopher was initially placed with them. They were increasingly beginning to draw parallels between the information they had received about the birth father and Christopher's aggressive behaviour.

Confusion around the impact of birth history/ genetic identity and identity formation

Supporting the parents

In supporting families when adolescents are struggling to make sense of their emerging identity, it is important to be aware that parents will often hold parallel fears to those of the young person. Christopher's parents were able to acknowledge their fears that his behaviour may be genetically linked to his birth father's difficulties. For many parents though, this can be an underlying fear that they do not quite recognize themselves or feel too uncomfortable admitting to. In my experience, being aware of this possibility and accepting it is very important. Siegel writes in *Brainstorm*[6] about the value in naming feelings as a way of reducing potentially overwhelming emotional states (calming the amygdala and activating the prefrontal cortex). Adoptive parents do wonder about the extent to which their child's 'genetic identity' will influence their personality. When birth parents have been destructive and frightening, this question can be one that generates a great deal of fear. Naming and normalizing these questions and fears is important in helping parents to consider the meaning of their child's behaviour from a more rational perspective. It isn't, after all, surprising that parents hold fears about their child's developing identity when they witness their increasingly worrying behaviours and think back to the information they received about their child's birth history when their child was placed with them. One of the most important elements in supporting parents to understand what is happening for their child is to help them understand the impact of trauma on development and to explore the nature vs. nurture debate. One of the common contributory factors to adoptive parents' fearful perception of their child's birth family is the information they receive about the birth family in official reports prior to the adoption. The very nature of these reports focuses on the difficulties within the birth families and the damaging and negative impact of their behaviours. Social services are understandably focused on the difficulties within birth families, as the task of removing children from the birth parents requires the case for significant harm to the child to be evidenced. It is, of course, important that the reality of the child's experience is documented and that there is a realistic and frank account of the harm that they suffered. Sometimes, though, there is insufficient exploration of the historical contributory factors that led to the birth parents becoming the individuals they were. In my experience, it is almost always the case that those birth parents who end up causing harm to their child, have themselves had extensive experiences within their own childhoods that have impacted negatively on their ability to parent safely. Sometimes, of course, parents may have failed to keep their children safe because of their addiction to drugs or alcohol or involvement in violent relationships. There may be no immediate evidence of childhood trauma available for these parents, but it is often likely that, in scratching the surface, earlier difficulties become apparent.

It is important that parents are given the opportunity to reflect on what led to the birth parents behaving in the way in which they did. To do so enables parents to understand the wider context of the birth parents as individuals and their likely developmental paths. Remaining open to considering the influences that impacted on the birth parent's life helps parents to hold in mind the fact that the birth parent was not 'born bad', that their destiny was not genetically predetermined any more than their child's is. Many birth parents will not have had the opportunity for respite from or support with very damaging earlier experiences. If they had, it may in many cases have been the case that they would not have ended up in the position they did. An appreciation of this can provide a hopeful message for adoptive parents, as their child won't have been exposed to many of the ongoing traumas that birth parents were before they reached adulthood. Within this message is a communication that their child can be different, that the different influences and quality of emotional life they have experienced within their adoptive family will make a difference to their development throughout the teenage years (no matter how much their current behaviour may be indicating otherwise). Behaviours that mirror those of birth parents do not necessarily represent a 'genetic victory' over their child's developing identity. If adoptive parents are able to keep this message in mind, they are much more likely to be able to communicate it clearly to their child. We are, after all, as much the sum of the experiences we haven't had as those we have had in life.

If parents are able to hold these messages in mind, they will be able to communicate them to their child. This is important (and not just for parents but for also others involved with adopted adolescents). Siegel states that:

> Unfortunately, what others believe about us can shape how we see ourselves and how we behave. This is especially true when it comes to teens and how they 'receive' commonly held negative attitudes that many adults project… Adolescents who are absorbing negative messages about who they are and what is expected of them may sink to that level instead of realizing their true potential.[7]

We have to give teenagers who hold confusion and fear in relation to their own developing identity and their perception of their genetic identity a message that they are not 'out of control' and heading towards a predetermined destiny.

Supporting the young person

Much of the work in supporting young people in untangling these complex questions is a parallel process to the work that needs to take place to support adoptive parents. Exploration of the reality of the young person's experience within their birth family, their understanding of who their birth parents are and the influences on their lives, the nature vs. nurture debate and the young person's understanding of the process of identity formation that they are going through are all important in increasing understanding for the young person and reducing fears. One of the most effective ways to incorporate all of these themes for adopted young people and their parents is to undertake therapeutic life-story work.

Chapters One, Three and Five explored the potential for making sense of one's history to support the healthy integration of the brain in addressing emotional and behavioural challenges and supporting the possibility of moving towards secure attachments. It can also be particularly helpful as a therapeutic process within which the young person can explore their early history and the meaning of this for their own identity formation whilst receiving supportive messages from their adoptive parents. Rose and Philpot[8] describe life-story work as being valuable in potentially providing the following in relation to identity formation:

- It supports the child to develop a sense of self.

- It gives a child a context within which to understand themselves and their world.

- It provides context and meaningful explanation to traumatic experiences.

- It can help to give the young person direction for their future life.

- It can help to demystify birth family and the past.

- It can provide clarity to missing links in information.

- It can help a child to move on.

• • • • • CHRISTOPHER – LIFE-STORY WORK • • • • •

Like the work undertaken with some of the other young people in previous chapters, the life-story work with Christopher provided an acceptance of his feelings and the opportunity to explore what these meant for him in relation to his sense of developing identity. The therapist, in being curious about Christopher's belief that he was headed towards a 'predetermined destiny' helped him to identify the very scary feelings that he held about this. Christopher was also able to express a sense of hopelessness within this belief. Christopher's painful feelings about a lack of contact from his birth father were also validated; although Christopher was very aware of his birth father's violence, he still grieved for the fact that he did not have a connection with him and held painful feelings that he thought his father didn't care about him because of this. Exploration was given to the detail of Christopher's early history and he was helped to understand the impact of these experiences on his current difficulties in regulating his emotions. The nature vs. nurture debate was also discussed, which helped Christopher to make sense of some of his confusion and more fearful fantasies about who he was in the present and would become in the future. Because Christopher's parents had been given the opportunity to work through their own questions and feelings prior to the work beginning with Christopher, they were able to support him in this with an openness and in an emotionally regulated way.

• •

Professional support is, of course, important when young people are really struggling with behaviours that may be related to struggles in their emerging identity but (as with the approaches discussed in Chapter Three) there is much that parents can do during this and earlier stages of development to support their young person with forming a positive identity. If parents are aware of the complexities that can arise in this area for adopted young people they can be alert to any indications that may suggest the young person is struggling. An openness to talking about the young person's history and the meaning of this for them is also crucial (and from the earliest stages of placement whenever possible). Young people are much more likely to instigate questions that they may have if these are part of an ongoing conversation that they can dip in and out of as they move through different developmental stages. Other opportunities can also arise to discuss the nurture vs. nature debate in daily life, as these themes are often present in television programmes, films and books. Addressing questions in this way can be a useful 'step removed' way of approaching the subject. Contact can also provide an excellent opportunity to make sense of the young person's birth history, what they understand of their birth parents and who they are within the context of this (contact will be discussed in Chapter Eight).

Identity and the risk of divided loyalty

Some adoptive parents worry that if the birth family identity is important to the young person there will be a risk that he or she will reject them as parents. This is an understandable worry, and the fear of loss is a very real one for parents. My experience is that young people may go through different stages in identifying strongly with birth family during adolescence. This is not a fixed stance though. Teenagers will often need to swing between different feelings as they make sense of their adoptive identity. It is a process that can take time and it's often not until late adolescence that the young person can integrate these different aspects of their identity.

Young people will often struggle with concerns about divided loyalties if they feel that both their birth and adoptive identities are important to them. If adoptive parents are able to be open to and accepting of it, the young person is much more likely to be able to confide in them and use their support to make sense of their developing identity. It is possible for young people to come to a secure resolution about their conflicting feelings:

> I used to get confused about who I called mum for a while, I would say 'this mum' and 'that mum'. They are both mum.

> I'm not 'just like her' and I'm not 'just like them'. I'm just me.

Conclusion

Struggles with identity formation can be very challenging for adopted teenagers and their parents; the process is, though, an important one and can carry huge benefits if navigated successfully. Families may well require additional support in relation to this area but there is much opportunity for a number of emotional needs to be met in doing so.

Parents I have worked with have provided the following observations and advice in thinking about this key theme.

On identity development as a 'normal' part of adolescence

Try and understand the 'normal' stuff about teenagers and identity – sometimes it's hard to distinguish between 'normal run of the mill teenage stuff' and the 'adoption stuff'. If they are rejecting your views, ideas of how they should be, being critical of how you live, your aspirations, etc. it's easy to panic that it's because they are adopted. It is part of being a teenager.

On receiving appropriate support

Use the training available out there about developmental trauma, for me that helped to place his behaviours in a wider context than my fears about who he was becoming in relation to his birth family.

Find the right support, the agency I used had a very different approach to our CAMH service. The therapeutic life-story work meant we were all involved in thinking about his story together. It joined it all up, connected it all. We thought about the meaning of it all together. I was surprised about how much he had to say about us that was positive and I also started to understand how important they [the birth family] still were to him.

On the importance of self-reflection

I think that you really need to be honest about yourself in relation to your views about the birth family. It's a difficult line to walk, I am clear that I don't condone what happened. I tell her that if I had been her mum then there is no way that I would have let those things happen to her. I am honest about my feelings that she was badly let down. At the same time I try and give a message of understanding them as people within their own context and experiences. If I was judgemental I think she would just cut me out of her own feelings about it.

You might need your own therapeutic support in coming to terms with your own fears and other feelings about what you are seeing in your child.

Chapter Seven

PEER RELATIONSHIPS AND EARLY INTIMATE RELATIONSHIPS

Peer relationships and early intimate relationships are an important part of the adolescent experience. This chapter will explore the central role and potential benefits that these relationships outside of the family provide for adolescents whilst also exploring the challenges that can arise for adopted young people in managing these relationships. The impact of these challenges on parents will be discussed and potential approaches and strategies for managing these challenges explored.

The importance and potential benefits of peer relationships in adolescence

Many adults, when reflecting on their adolescence, will recall the friendships they experienced during these years. Intense, complex, novel, conflictual, joyous, poignant, passionate, vibrant, frustrating, confusing, loving, chaotic and meaningful are just some of the words used by adults when I asked them to describe friendship during this stage of life. The meaning of friendship in teenage years, with the particular quality and intensity that those relationships carry, is often easily recalled by those looking back across the decades. This is true for those recalling a painful absence of friendship and difficult times with peer groups or for those reminiscing about wonderful friendships, perhaps not experienced in quite the same way since. The placement of the experience of friendship as a central part of the experience of adolescence was pertinent to all of the adults I spoke to when discussing their teenage years. When we consider the reasons for this, it is easy to understand why.

Our peer relationships in teenage years are particularly important to us because they provide a number of important functions during this developmental stage. The quality of mind of 'social engagement' primes the adolescent brain for an increased need to engage with others socially, enhance peer connections and create new friendships. As adolescents we *need* to do this. In 'pulling away' from our primary attachments with our parents, friendships can provide a safe and inclusive home of meaningful and protective relationships. Birsch writes in *Teenagers and Attachment*:

> Detachment or separation from the family is made possible by groups of adolescents that present themselves as a new and accepting 'emotional safe haven', in place of the security of the dyadic attachment (that is, pair-bond') represented by the primary attachment figure. Groups enable the adolescent to explore the world: enter, for the first time, into intimate relationships with others and, embark on other adventures, without necessarily gaining the consent of parental attachment figures. The young person's peers provide crucial support and encouragement. The feeling of safety in the adolescent group has a similar fear-reducing effect as did the sense of emotional security with the early attachment figure.[1]

It is a survival strategy to connect more with peers – a safety net for when, as teenagers, we begin the separation process from our parents. Friendships can provide a safer base to novelty seeking in the increasingly wider world – comrades in arms in new adventures, exploring alongside us and sharing new experiences.

These relationships outside of the family are also an important part of identity development. Through our peers' eyes we begin increasingly to make sense of our emerging identities: who are we, where do we fit, with whom do we identify, what is their experience of us and us them?

They begin to simultaneously compare their evaluation of their own attributes with the evaluations that they believe several others hold of them.[2]

It is only in adolescent life that we choose distinct identities and group identities to belong to through peer relationships in quite this way. At any point in contemporary culture teenagers have defined themselves within distinct identities and often in opposition to one another depending on their 'chosen group': mods vs. rockers, emos vs. hip hop enthusiasts, populars vs. alternatives, swots vs. rebels, the sporty kids vs. the grungy kids, Oasis fans vs. Blur fans and so on and so on and so on. It would be highly unusual (although perhaps more than a little amusing) to find adults in the workplace grouped around the water cooler in the separate uniforms of their chosen identities, using slang and cultural references to reinforce those identities in quite the same way (although of course some would argue that this continues in a subtler and more nuanced way throughout life).

Through friendships adolescents embark upon new adventures, make sense of themselves, forge strong bonds and divisions, relate to the wider world around them and form a world away from the family relationships on which they had previously been primarily dependent. What, though, happens for young people who struggle with relationships? Many adopted teenagers, as we have seen, experience significant difficulties with attachment relationships; these difficulties will often translate to their capacity to form close and supportive bonds with friends and peer groups at a time when they are particularly important for their ongoing development.

Potential challenges in peer-group relationships for adopted teenagers

Many adopted teenagers will bring their difficulties with attachment relationships to their peer relationships. Parents may well observe that their children's attachment behaviour within the family home is replicated within their relationships in their wider social circle. Birsch[3] highlights the way in which different insecure attachment patterns can 'play out' within peer-group relationships. He highlights the tendency for young people with an insecure-avoidant attachment style to use peer groups for shared activities and exploration, whilst at the same time struggling to engage in emotional relationships within the group. The emotional impact of this for the young person is that their engagement in the group will tend to be shallow and lacking in emotional commitment, with little expectation of emotional support from the friendships. Friends are likely to experience the young person as emotionally detached and perhaps as feeling less 'authentic' in their relationships. The young person is unable to use these relationships to form meaningful emotional support whilst at the same time detaching from their families.[4] The resulting impact can be that the adolescent is left with a feeling of detachment and loneliness, unable to experience meaningful emotional support during this crucial stage. Teenagers who have an insecure-ambivalent attachment style are likely to relate to their peers in a way that may feel overwhelming for their peers. Their underlying fears of insecurity and being abandoned are likely to lead to intense but conflictual relationships. They may move between intense fluctuations between group and individual activities. When away from the peer group the young person can feel insecure, worrying that they are 'unseen and not heard' but once back within the group will experience high levels of anxiety and unmet need. The peer group is likely to experience the young person's behaviour as confusing, perhaps disloyal and unreliable in meeting their respective emotional needs. The young person who is struggling in this way will not experience the benefits of consistent support from their friends and will experience the relationships as stressful.

Those young people who have an insecure-disorganized attachment style will behave in a disorganized way within their peer relationships. Friends will find their behaviours and emotions hard to understand. The young person's responses to peers can fluctuate quickly between seeking closeness and feeling stifled, resulting in belligerent accusations and even violence towards the group. The peer group is likely to experience the young person as dramatic and unpredictable, even scary. Whilst some peers may empathize with these young people, many will reject them and friendship groups may well find themselves 'split' because of the impact of the young person's attachment behaviour. The young person is likely to find the whole experience of friendship frustrating, confusing and completely lacking in emotional meaning and support.[5]

The consequences of these struggles for teenagers mean that they are unlikely to benefit from the emotional support and safety net that they need as they move through the process of separation from their parents. Experiencing difficulties in peer relationships whilst also struggling in their attachment relationships with parents can be very distressing for adopted adolescents. They can feel disconnected and disorientated.

Teenagers are all too aware of their shortcomings within their peer groups, as their adolescent brains are so highly attuned in awareness to this area.

In Chapter Five I considered some of the ways in which parents could support their teenagers in using their relationships with them for effective emotional support during this stage. Unfortunately, these considerations are less straightforward when we are considering ways of supporting the young person within their relationships with peers. The young person's peers are unlikely to be well equipped to understand the emotional needs underlying the young person's attachment behaviours and are less likely to be tolerant of their difficulties. There are, though, a number of approaches and strategies that parents can employ that may be useful in supporting the young person with friendships during this stage.

- If parents understand that their teenager's difficulties in this area are located in very real challenges in being able to engage successfully in relationships, they can help to provide the message of these difficulties being a matter of 'can't do' rather than 'won't do' both for themselves and the young person. This can help to adjust the parents' and teenager's expectations of what they are able to manage at this stage and perhaps avoid repeated experiences of trying to manage relationships that the teenager is not yet equipped to cope with. It can also support the parents in maintaining empathy for the young person (and therefore support the young person in maintaining empathy for the self). Making sense of why the young person struggles with peer relationships may help to reduce feelings of shame that the young person may carry about their difficulties in this area too.

- If young people struggle with peer relationships, parents may need to provide structured social opportunities so that the young person is able to experience peer interaction in a successful way. Social time that is structured and supervised by adults with clear expectations can help to reduce anxiety and limit the unsupervised peer interactions that are much more nuanced and harder to negotiate. If adolescents have particular interests that can be pursued in group settings, this of course does make it much easier.

We have found that the only activities our daughter can manage well with peers are those that are structured by an adult. It may not be exactly what her friends are doing but at least if she is at her Guides group or dance class or Cadets she is mixing with peers who she feels are her friends. She isn't going to manage relationships with girls of her own age right now without it getting chaotic. Within a very structured environment though, she is experiencing social activities safely and also having an experience of positive social interaction.

- Parents have suggested that setting up friendships with older adolescents/young adults within their social networks can be useful for providing social outlets for young people who struggle. Older adolescents/young adults are likely to have the capacity for a better understanding of the young person's difficulties and more tolerance for them.

It can be really helpful if you have young people in your family or friends network who are in late adolescence or early adulthood who are willing to spend time with your children. We have found that this has worked really well for our sons who sometimes struggle with a lot of conflict within their relationships with their peer group. There is something about that gap in the developmental stage that means that they are much more able to tolerate our sons' difficulties and provide them with some social outlet. When they are with them we feel that we can relax, knowing that they are going to manage that time and get something positive from it.

Try to get him/her to talk to other people/maintain other relationships in the family. Young adults in the family can be really helpful.

Other features of adopted teenagers' peer relationships

Seeking out friendships that reflect the young person's struggle with their birth vs. adoptive identity

Chapter Six discussed the additional challenges that adopted teenagers can face in exploring and making sense of their identity. The friendships and peer groups that young people seek out in adolescence will also often reflect the various aspects of the young person's identity that they are trying to resolve. In my experience, young people will often seek out friendships with other young people who are adopted or who are in foster or residential care.

In many ways these relationships can provide a sense of shared identity. Young people can gain a great deal from being with other young people with whom they have a sense of shared experience. Within these relationships the young person doesn't feel as 'alone' or 'different' as they can do within their relationships with their peers who have not had similar experiences.

· · · · · · · · · REBECCA AGED 15 · · · · · · · · ·

Rebecca's relationships in earlier and mid childhood had, for the most part, been with those children within her parents' immediate social circle or with friends she met through school. As she moved further into adolescence she became much more aware of her early history within her birth family and the differences in her life experiences to those of the friends she had grown up with up until that point in her childhood. Whilst Rebecca was managing fairly well in coming to terms with her early history, she described her feelings of disconnection from her friends in their capacity to understand her own emotional experience as a result of her past and her adoption. She still valued these friendships but described a feeling of 'distance' from her close friends at times. She was dealing with some very powerful and complex feelings, which were inevitably preoccupying her at times. It was hard for her to talk to her friends about her experiences, as she felt that they didn't have any comprehension of them. At secondary school she met a new friend, another adopted young person, with whom she felt a very strong connection. This friendship was a very intense one for her; she was able to share her feelings with someone who had also 'been there'. Rebecca described this friendship as a 'shortcut' to someone who 'she got' and whom she felt 'got her'. It wasn't without its difficulties of course but the experience of being understood by a peer was understandably a very important experience for her.

These friendships can, however, create additional challenges for the young person. When teenagers identify with peers who are also struggling with very painful pasts (and experiencing difficulties in managing across a range of their behaviours in the present), they can find themselves feeling that it is inevitable that their life will continue on a downwards spiral. Some young people may conclude that all those who have experienced painful pasts will inevitably head towards a future that resembles that of their birth parents' world.

• • • • • • • • • STEPHEN AGED 14 • • • • • • • • • •

Stephen had been permanently excluded from school in year 8. His parents, recognizing that he was not going to be able to manage with mainstream school, had found him a placement for him in a specialist education project that combined practical training in mechanics with core GCSEs. Stephen was actually doing well at the project and had made a number of friendships, which had extended outside of the project. Stephen's new friends were also young people who were struggling in various parts of their lives and had been unable to manage mainstream education. For the majority of them, they were outside of the 'usual' pathways into adulthood. Involved in criminal behaviour and leading fairly chaotic lives, they had a shared sense of being different to the 'normal' teenagers worrying about exams and planning their futures. When Stephen's friends talked about their family lives he recognized many features (often involving domestic violence, chaotic parents, alcohol and drug abuse by family members) as being present within his own history within his birth family. Stephen had not been removed from his birth family until he was six years old and he still held many memories of the traumatic events he experienced with his birth mother. Stephen had reflected a great deal on this new peer group; none of his new friends were adopted but they had all experienced (and some were still experiencing) adverse family circumstances. In comparing his new friends with his other friends, Stephen had come to the conclusion that his new friends' path in life would inevitably be one of failure in education, followed by a path into criminality and a life outside that of the 'normal' people in society. Stephen only had two seemingly opposing examples of how life worked: if you came from a 'good' family and had a 'normal' life you would be pretty much fine, like (in his perception) most of the friends he had grown up with. If you had 'bad blood', a background that was full of adversity, you would take a completely different path in life. Stephen didn't have the capacity or wider experience of life to develop a more sophisticated understanding of what makes us who we are as human beings. The friendship group he was now identifying with reinforced all of his fantasies about the impact of his early history, what he understood about his birth family and what this meant for his own future identity.

Stephen needed help to make sense of his confusion and concerns in regard to his understanding of his own history, the impact of that history on his current struggles and what he was able to understand in relation to his observations of his peers' lives. Stephen was already engaged in therapeutic work and this was extended to include life-story work. Like Christopher in the preceding chapter, Stephen was given the opportunity to explore his questions of why we are who we are and how much control we have over our destinies. This process was greatly aided by exploring his understanding of his friends' lives. With help, Stephen was gradually able to develop a more sophisticated understanding of the many variables impacting on his and his friends' lives. But it was clear that his experience of friendships and starkly different peer groups had been a huge influence on his developing understanding of his own identity.

Forming friendships with others who are engaged with risky behaviour

Chapter Two discussed the developmentally appropriate drive to take risks in the adolescent years. The chapter also discussed the additional vulnerabilities that adopted teenagers will have in this area. Adolescents will often find peers who will engage in risk-taking behaviour with them. They may come into contact with other teenagers whose relationship with risk is similar to theirs in specialist education settings, through youth offending teams or just by engaging in risky behaviour in itself (the young person who is using drugs and alcohol and out late at night will invariably find other teenagers to share these experiences with!). Joining up with other teenagers who are engaging enthusiastically in risk-taking behaviour does, unfortunately, up the ante in regard to the young person's safety. Adolescents who are engaged in their own social world and on the edge of criminal and antisocial activities without the input of adults are much more likely to 'up' their risk-taking behaviour significantly. Young people in these circumstances are often at risk of becoming part of gangs or being groomed by older adolescents and adults into unsafe activities. Young people who are hyper vigilant to danger are often drawn to the illusion of safety that exists within gangs.

The advantage that adopted teenagers usually have in comparison to many of their peers in this type of grouping is that they have parents who are still working hard to be present in their lives and who represent an adult presence and 'interruption' in this peer-group dynamic. This is incredibly important to young people, even if they don't seem to appreciate it at the time! Many young people don't have any choice but to exist within extended peer groups without adult support. The adopted adolescent does. Even if their pull towards their peer group seems much stronger than their attachment relationships with their parents at times, it is absolutely worth parents' effort to maintain a presence in the young person's life. Continuing to offer the secure base for as long as is possible and providing a regulating and alternative voice are very important. Adolescents need adults in their lives.

The value of connecting with other adopted teenagers

There is value in young people having the opportunity to connect with other adopted teenagers within a group setting. Sharing experiences, exploring common themes and working through questions and feelings are all potentially beneficial for adopted adolescents.

I think that there should be more opportunity to get together with other teenagers. I really liked the teenagers' group I went to but it didn't last long. It was really good to be with the others and talk about stuff. We had stuff in common that other kids our age can't really understand. It was really good to hear that the others had the same experiences as me. We could talk about what we thought about our birth families. With them I was 'normal' not different.

Bringing young people together who also share complex difficulties can also of course carry risks; as I have already discussed, these difficulties can combine and up the ante in regard to riskier behaviours. Groups need to be well managed and staffed by experienced professionals. There also needs to be the capacity for following up issues that arise within group settings for young people afterwards.

A note on the additional challenges of social media

For teenagers who are struggling with peer relationships, a key part of the adolescent's peer/social life, social media, can be almost impossible to navigate safely and can make life yet still more challenging. This can be because the ever-present nature of social media means there is very little possibility for a break from social interaction. In Get Out of My Life... But First Take Me and Alex Into Town, Wolf and Franks write:

> With the ever increasing role of the electronic world in their lives, teenagers feel connected to a network of peers. Of course, in the not too distant past there was television (although comparatively fewer channels and only available during specified limited hours) and teenagers could always chat on their house phone. But aside from this, once the family was together at home there was not this permanent sense of connection to the word outside, especially through

constant texting and web-surfing. Today it is as if the walls of the home are porous. Home is no longer a sanctuary from the wider world![6]

It also, however, presents a number of challenges for adopted young people who struggle with difficulties such as: impulsiveness, problems managing sexual boundaries, vulnerability to exploitation by other young people and adults and issues with managing their emotional regulation. Parents have reported a range of behaviours in relation to social media that have caused them great anxiety and concern. In my experience, these behaviours have included: 'sexting' (when young people have sent naked photos of themselves to peers) and sometimes these images have then been shared with others via social media; angry outbursts from the young person via social media, which have then caused them a great deal of trouble (either from disgruntled adults or other teenagers eager to retaliate); a lack of ability to evaluate potentially harmful contacts and behaviours from others via social media; 'over sharing' information on social media; and bullying via social media. Many adolescents simply don't have the necessary degree of emotional regulation and understanding to navigate peer relationships in the way in which social media requires them to. The perception of being 'more distant' than they actually are from those on the receiving end of their interaction via social media can disinhibit impulses in young people who already struggle in inhibiting their emotional responses. As we know, the teenage brain is also predisposed to evaluating the likelihood of a positive outcome, even when evidence points to the contrary. It is easy to see why sending risky photographs in an attempt to please a boyfriend/girlfriend can be too tempting and likely to be enacted without thought of the potential consequences of such actions.

Managing the impact of social media on young people's lives is very challenging. Previous advice given to parents about ensuring that young people only used the family computer within the home (so that parents could monitor their internet use) is less valid now that teenagers have handheld devices (often within their phones). It is, though, still advisable to provide breaks in teenagers' social media use whenever this is possible. This provides a respite for the adolescent in the face of the intensity of these demands (adolescents find it incredibly difficult to put pauses in place themselves; the quality of mind of social engagement is a very powerful drive!). Sometimes it may be possible for parents to enforce breaks.

> I have a rule that phones are off when we have dinner and also take her phone out of her bedroom when it's time for her to sleep. It gives, I hope, at least a short respite every day when she's not feeling that intense sense of connection to those networks.

Sometimes parents may need to take the opportunity where it arises, for example, when they manage to engage the young person in an activity (such as playing sports or whilst at the cinema).

It can also be beneficial to maintain an open, ongoing conversation about some of the downsides of social media risks and, if possible, to talk about the particular vulnerabilities the young person may have in managing these risks.

> I make sure I am very clear about the possible risks of social media with her. The school does do assemblies about this but whenever I read something about risks I talk to her about it. I also talk with her about why she particularly may find it difficult to manage some of the applications she uses. She is impulsive and can do really silly things in an attempt to impress friends. I'm sure she finds it all highly irritating but

I live in hope that she'll remember some of the conversations and be able to use the advice.

The impact of difficulties in peer relationships for parents

Whilst there is no doubt that peer relationships can be very challenging for many adopted teenagers, there is also no doubt, in my experience, that these difficulties can prove very challenging for the parents who are trying to support them. Parents report that their children's difficulties in this area present a number of emotional challenges for them.

- For many parents their young people's difficulties in being able to form and maintain healthy peer relationships is another reminder of the 'differences' in their developmental path compared with other young people. The additional support that their children need in this area can feel overwhelming for parents who are already having to try and meet their additional needs in other areas of their lives.

- Parents also experience feelings of grief about the lack of the potentially joyous aspects of teenage years that their child isn't having because of their difficulties with friendships.

- Many parents will experience high degrees of anxiety in relation to the choices that their teenagers are making about with whom they are friends and with whom they identify. Worries about safety are, of course, paramount. Whilst the parents of any adolescent will lie awake worrying about if their son or daughter is OK, this fear takes on another level of intensity when the parent is aware that their child's choice of friends significantly ups the ante in regard to risky behaviour.

- Parents worry, too, about the meaning of chosen friendships in relation to their child's emerging identity. Just as the young person will experience confusion and try and make sense of their identity via their peer relationships, so too will their parents. The choosing of risky peer relationships can amplify the sense that the young person is rejecting every value their parents tried to install in them in their childhood and instead turning to those values and acquaintances who reflect the child's birth history.

- If young people are simply not managing peer relationships because of their insecure attachment styles, they are not able to access the potential emotional benefits of those peer relationships. The balance of what the young person still needs to seek from their parents at home (during a developmental stage when they would usually be fulfilling at least part of this need outside of the home) can cause a great deal of emotional pressure for parents and conflict within the home.

• • • • • • • • • • • KATHERINE • • • • • • • • • • •

Katherine is an adoptive mother to her 16-year-old son, Richard, a young man who struggles with peer relationships. His emotional developmental stage is much younger than his chronological age and he tends towards an avoidant style in his attachment relationships. Richard finds it difficult to find common ground with his peer group and they generally find it difficult to relate to him. He also suffers from high levels of anxiety and as a consequence often finds it difficult to leave the home. Katherine empathizes with her son's difficulties and she and her husband have worked hard to try and provide structured activities for Richard outside of the home. The impact of Richard's isolation on family life is, though, still extremely stressful for Katherine. Katherine describes her own feelings of frustration and sense of being 'trapped' within her own home at times because of her son's inability to form relationships or attend activities outside of the home. The intensity of Richard's constant presence combined with his own feelings of frustration and conflicting feelings arising from his continuing dependence on his parents, whilst still experiencing the need to 'be separate' from them, makes for an often explosive atmosphere within the home. Katherine understands that there is simply 'no one else' for Richard to direct his frustration towards, but the intensity of the relationship can feel overwhelming for both her and her husband. She acknowledges that her own feelings of grief in regard to the childhood that Richard has not had because of his early experiences have resurfaced 'anew' for her during this stage of her son's adolescence. The reality of the extent of his struggles with peer relationships and the fear that he may never achieve a successful independent life with successful adult relationships is, at times, overwhelming for Katherine and her husband.

A lack of social outlets and peer relationships for young people can also mean that parents of adopted teenagers don't benefit from the natural 'breaks' within the parent–child relationship that a social life outside of the home can afford. For parents who are already managing high levels of need for their children this can place a great deal of additional pressure on them. 'Natural' opportunities for respite from challenging relationships within the home are simply not available when there is a lack of opportunity for relationships that can be healthy and supportive outside of the home.

When reflecting on managing this challenging time, parents have observed the following as strategies they have found useful.

I do sometimes get really frustrated that he can't do it [have a social life] but I remind myself that it's definitely a case of 'can't do rather than won't do'. It does help me to retain my sympathy and therefore patience with him.

I invite his friends into our home, even if I don't like them or am worried about their influence on him. Maybe it's a case of 'better the devil you know' but it gives me some sense of control, having some awareness of what they are doing, what they are talking about and keeps a connection in his mind I think between us and his 'outside world'.

One of the hardest things in teenage years when it comes to friendships is that you don't know who their parents are and often don't have any contact details for them or their families. I always try to take a mobile number from one of her friends if they are going out for the evening 'just in case of emergencies'. It means I have a store of numbers I can call if I can't get hold of her as well. I've also found that when parents are around in the picture they are usually open to communication as well so whenever I can I try and make those links.

I make sure that I maintain my own friendships and social outlets wherever I can. If you have a child who is struggling it can feel overwhelming and it's easy to think I'm too tired/ it's too much hassle to go out or meet with people. It really is so important for my wellbeing though; otherwise I could end up feeling as isolated as him and then that's both of us in the same dark place!

As a parent to a now young adult my advice in looking back on some her friendship choices would be to try and hold in mind that many of these alliances will be temporary in their nature. Friends come and go according to where they 'are at' in themselves in different stages of development. These choices do change over time and eventually I think they do start to make wiser choices for themselves. I think with adopted young people that it can just take a lot longer.

You can't control who your child chooses as friends in the teenage years! By all means keep your boundaries clear in relation to what is acceptable within your home and your expectations of your child but don't waste a lot of energy and get into yet more conflict in trying to control their friendships. Believe me, it achieves very little except additional stress!

Early intimate relationships

The majority of adolescents are likely to enter their first romantic and sexual relationships in the teenage years. The drive to connect with others is a powerful one and the way in which teenagers will manage these early intimate relationships is dependent upon a number of influences including temperament, family, friends and culture.[7] Navigating these early intimate relationships is often not easy for teenagers. We live in a culture within which teenagers are exposed to complex messages in regard to sexual behaviour and sexual identity. Teenagers of both genders will often experience confusion in understanding what is safe and healthy sexual behaviour, and cultural messages in relation to sexual identity are often constructed around other elements of identity including class, religion, race and sexual orientation. There simply isn't the space to explore developing sexuality and these early romantic relationships fully within this chapter; instead I would like to focus on some of the particular challenges for adopted adolescents that often arise as being part of the reason that parents seek support from services.

*The particular challenges for adopted adolescents in
entering into intimate and sexual relationships*

I have already discussed the ways in which insecure attachment
styles will influence young people's abilities to use parent and
peer relationships during adolescence. Those same difficulties
will apply to romantic relationships, with young people
demonstrating those avoidant, ambivalent or disorganized
attachment strategies in trying to manage their fears and
vulnerabilities. Romantic relationships (like peer relationships)
are more reciprocal in nature, with both parties having a
similar level of need of one another. Like peer relationships,
partners in romantic relationships may be less tolerant of the
young person's more complex attachment behaviours. Their
need for the relationship is different and their responses are
likely to reflect this. These relationships may therefore prove
to be very challenging for those young people with less secure
attachment styles.

The impact of earlier traumatic experiences can also
come to the fore in adolescence as young people experience
a new intensity of sexual feelings and/or engage in their first
sexual relationships. Earlier experiences of sexual abuse may
be brought to the surface and young people may experience
a number of responses to this; they may feel that their body
has no value or control. There is sometimes a risk that those
young people may move into behaviours that 're-enact' those
early experiences. Some young people may engage in unsafe,
promiscuous encounters for example, dissociating from their
emotional states as they re-enact earlier experiences. If parents
are concerned about their young person's sexual behaviour and
they are aware that there was (or there possibly was) sexual
abuse in the young person's background, it is important to seek
therapeutic support. An increase in the intensity and frequency
of sexual feelings can feel very scary for young people who
have experienced earlier abuse. They are unlikely to be able to

recognize that unhealthy sexual behaviour in adolescence may be a response to this.

Young people may also struggle to make sense of romantic relationships and sexual behaviour within the context of their wider identity exploration. Many adopted teenagers will be aware of differences between their birth parents' and adopted parents' approaches to behaviours within relationships with their respective partners. Some teenagers' explorations of their feelings within their own relationships may be confused by their attempts to integrate those wider questions of 'Who am I like?' In earlier chapters I have discussed the importance of untangling these questions and beliefs with young people (whether this is via discussions with parents or in life-story work with professionals) in order to 'make sense of' fears and fantasies. This is equally important in helping young people make sense of the way they behave in these romantic relationships. Young people who do engage in unhealthy sexual behaviours may assume that they are simply 'like their birth parent' (if this was present in their birth parent's behaviour). This can increase worrying feelings of a lack of control for the young person.

Other young people may struggle in this area because of the difficulties they experience in some of the areas I discussed in the first three chapters. Impulsivity, poorly developed empathy, poorly developed cause and effect, a high level of need for control, low self-esteem, difficulties in connecting with others and the qualities of mind of increased emotional intensity and creative exploration are particularly likely to influence the young person's capacity to make moderated and well-judged choices. Some young people will be particularly vulnerable to predatory behaviour from abusive adults because they struggle to understand the intent and motivation of others. Some young people may be at risk themselves of engaging in abusive behaviour because of difficulties in the above areas. All of these challenges are, of course, being navigated within the context of a culture that can actively promote the kind of sexual behaviour that is more about the casual 'hook up' as opposed to sexual behaviour within the context of safe and nurturing relationships.

This is an extremely complex area and a very challenging one for parents to respond to. I would like to conclude this chapter by turning to the range of feelings and fears that parents often express about their young person's sexual behaviour. Some of these include the following:

- Shame: parents' views about morality and fear of judgment by others can be triggered by their young person's behaviour and it can be a struggle to not convey these feelings to the young person.

  > I was just horrified and her dad couldn't cope with it at all; it was just excruciatingly embarrassing. To have to see those images, awkward wasn't the word. (A mother talking about being shown images of her daughter's 'sexts')

- Fear of pregnancy: this is often a profound fear for adoptive parents. The risk of unplanned pregnancy is a very real one when young people are engaged in unsafe sexual behaviour. The majority of adolescents with significant emotional difficulties risk history 'repeating itself' if they progress with pregnancies before they are able to manage this. Parents worry that the pattern of social services involvement (which may have occurred across multiple generations of the birth family) will continue into their child's experience. Parents express fear that the young person's own child could end up being removed into foster care. Parents also worry that they will be placed in the position of having to take on the care of the child in order to prevent this; many parents (already stretched to their limits) recognize that they may not be able to do this. Some parents worry that their child is in some way seeking to have a baby, and this may be the case. Young people who are struggling with loss and unresolved feelings about their early history may seek to address these feelings by having a baby of their own.

Approaching worrying sexual behaviours is challenging for parents. It isn't possible to control the young person's sexual behaviour but it may be useful to adopt the following approaches in influencing the young person.

- Communicate concern about behaviour on the basis of physical and emotional safety. Approaching the issue as a moralistic one is only likely to increase feelings of shame and close down any opportunity for exploration and reflection on the young person's part. Parents do need to be attentive to any feelings they may hold that are shame based, as these are likely to be communicated to the young person.

- Think in terms of the 'emotional detective' stance; why is the young person behaving in this way, how may their behaviour be linked to their wider difficulties and are there any features of their early experience that may lead to particular challenges in this area for them?

- Adopt the PACE stance in exploring this with the young person; communicate concerns as emanating from a place of concern for the young person's wellbeing, accept that there will be reasons that they are struggling in this area, be curious about their experience of the way in which they are behaving and empathetic to their struggle.

- Seek professional support if the young person can be open to this. Approaching the need for support on the basis of the young person's sexual behaviour is only likely to increase shame for the young person, but placing the behaviour within the wider context of other areas of concern may be less threatening for them. Support that is adoption-focused is likely to be most beneficial.

- If possible, speak with other parents of adopted teenagers. Difficulties in this area are very common for adoptive families; sharing this experience and receiving support and advice from those who have 'been there and got the t-shirt' can be very useful and help to reduce the parents' own feelings of shame.

Finally, I do think that it is important to hold in mind the fact that there are many influences on the way in which young people manage their sexuality. The cultural messages around this are very muddled and confusing for young people. Some secondary schools do provide education in relation to developing healthy relationships in adolescence, and there are some local schemes around the country that aim to promote safety and awareness for young people in managing relationships. It is always worth contacting your local post-adoption team to check which services are available and what is provided within the young person's school curriculum. Whilst psycho-education in itself won't necessarily address the young person's difficulties a 'drip, drip' approach to reflecting on and exploring relationships (from sources other than parents) can be useful for young people.

CONTACT AND THE ADOLESCENT YEARS

Contact with birth family members during the teenage years is often identified as one of the primary concerns for adoptive parents. The adolescent years often bring a new focus to contact issues for a variety of reasons.

- The adopted teenager is much more likely to be curious about their birth family identity at this stage of development (the quality of mind of 'creative exploration').

- The adopted teenager may well be struggling with managing profound and complex feelings of loss in relation to their birth family at this stage of development (the quality of mind of 'emotional intensity').

- The adopted teenager is likely to have access to social media (particularly Facebook) at this time. Contact with birth family members may be 'one click away' on the keyboard, something that is very difficult to inhibit with the teenager's 'novelty seeking' and 'social engagement' qualities of mind.

- The adopted teenager is likely to be more impulsive and to anticipate the outcomes of any risk in making contact with their birth family to be balanced in their favour at this stage of their development (hyper rational thinking).

- The adopted teenager will be moving into the process of individuation and separation at this stage of their development and will be managing anxiety around changes in their relationship with their adoptive parents.

Contact arrangements to date

Many adopted teenagers will have had contact arrangements in place with birth family members prior to adolescence. These arrangements are most commonly in the form of letterbox contact arrangements and may involve an either/or combination of letter exchanges between the adoptive family and the birth family. Some arrangements include the exchange of photographs and even video footage of adopted children. In much rarer circumstances, young people have had ongoing direct contact with birth family members; this is most likely to take place between siblings but does sometimes happen with birth parents and other extended family members. Some young people may have received contact from birth family members in the earlier stages of their childhood but these arrangements may have tailed off over time.

The potential benefits of contact

Ongoing contact arrangements may have worked well for adopted young people up until their teenage years. In my experience, there can be a number of positive factors in maintaining contact with the birth family if it is able to fulfil a number of important functions, which are listed below.

The potential for letterbox contact to support the child's
understanding of their birth or 'genetic' identity

Often there is an assumption that this can be achieved purely through the process of contact taking place. In my experience, this is often not the case within letterbox communication, as it may only give a general overview of what the birth family member has been doing since the last contact exchange. It is possible to support this area if there is an active dialogue between the adoptive parents and the young person as to their experience of the information they have received, which enables them to ask questions to help them make sense of the contact exchange. This may simply be a case of the adoptive parent 'wondering about' what impression, feelings or questions the letter raises for the young person. An example of this would be the adoptive parent wondering aloud about this within the context of the information received within the letter. This can open up a dialogue between the parent and young person that helps them to make sense of the birth parent as a whole beyond the scope of the letter. Sometimes, an attuned adoptive parent can use their observations of the way in which their child responds to letterbox contact to increase their understanding of their birth parent further.

• • • • • • • • • • STEVEN AGED 12 • • • • • • • • • • •

A lovely example of this occurred within a letterbox exchange I managed for a 12-year-old boy, Steven, who had been adopted by his foster carers. Steven had twice-yearly letterbox contact with his birth mother. Steven had been removed from his birth mother at the age of seven years because she was unable to care for him safely as a result of her drug and alcohol abuse. Steven's memories of his life with his birth mother were of a chaotic existence in which he was sometimes left alone, often did not have enough to eat and was sometimes on the receiving end of explosive temper tantrums from his mother. Steven's birth mother had apologized to Steven for her lack of care and had shown genuine remorse that she had frightened him and neglected him in the past. She had accepted the plan for Steven to be adopted as her own health deteriorated, and had been reassured that he was to be adopted by his foster carers. She had had some direct contact with Steven with his foster carers in the early stages of his placement but this had not been a positive experience for Steven, as her addiction problems had meant that she was inconsistent in her attendance. Social services had subsequently recommended that the plan for contact should be via the letterbox system only and she eventually accepted this with the support of her drugs and alcohol worker who had been an independent counsellor for her for some time. She was able to be consistent in her letterbox letters, showed pride in Steven's achievements and clearly missed him.

Steven looked forward to her letters but often showed a great deal of angry behaviour after receiving them. Steven's adoptive mother was sensitive enough to note that Steven had conflicting feelings in relation to the contact, and after sharing one contact with him she talked with him about this. She explained to Steven that she had noticed he liked receiving these letters but that they also made him angry and, she suspected, more than a little bit sad. She wondered with him about whether there was anything she could do to help figure out how to help him with these feelings. Steven was able to articulate his feeling that it made him angry that his birth mother could write nice letters to him but that she didn't love him enough to look after him properly when he lived with her. He wondered if she was 'pretending' in the letters or whether she had changed enough to be able to look after him but didn't want him back. Steven could explain that he sometimes thought his birth mother was a 'bad' person and that it didn't make sense to him that she could write nice letters but couldn't look after him.

Steven's adoptive mother contacted me to see if there was anything she could do to help Steven with these understandably confused feelings. I had met Steven's birth mother on a number of occasions and knew that, despite her difficulties, she genuinely cared for Steven and would like to help. I decided that it would be worth talking to her to see if, with support, she could help Steven to make more sense of her as a person and provide some explanation herself as to what had happened in her own life to create the difficulties that had led to her neglect of, and abusive behaviour towards, Steven.

During the meeting with Steven's birth mother I explained to her that I did not know much about her own life – that I knew things had gone badly wrong but not why. I asked her to talk to me about her own experiences as a child and if there was anything that she felt could help Steven to understand her better. What Steven's mother was able to explain was very moving and proved to be very beneficial for Steven. She explained that she felt her early childhood had been OK. She had grown up with her mother and sister until her mother had remarried when she was 11 years old. Her stepfather had been an extremely abusive man. She had witnessed her mother being badly physically assaulted on numerous occasions and she and her sister had regularly been beaten. By the time she was 13 years old she was escaping the nightmare at home by staying away as much as possible. She began drinking, slept wherever she could (often with risky adults) and began taking harder drugs in her later teens. She had naively believed when she became pregnant with Steven that she would be able to change and give him the kind of childhood she had wished for herself. She had not, though, been able to overcome her addictions; her lifestyle remained chaotic and she had found the demands of caring for Steven completely overwhelming. Her own health continued to be poor, her life expectancy was limited and she expressed a huge degree of shame and guilt that she had failed Steven so badly. When I asked her what she would like me to tell Steven about herself her words were: 'That I haven't always been like this, I wasn't born such a mess.' I asked her if she could tell me something about her earlier, happier childhood. What had she been like? What did she enjoy doing? She explained that she always asked Steven in her letters how his swimming was progressing. This was because she felt very proud of his clear talent and achievements in his competitive swimming, but also because she herself had competed in swimming competitions and had been very talented. She had loved swimming and gained a lot of self-esteem from competing and winning. She felt great that Steven had this too and was very proud of him.

I left the meeting with Steven's birth mother with a much better understanding of her as a person. Her story was moving and I had a clear sense of the girl that she once was before her life descended into chaos. I made an appointment to visit Steven and his adoptive parents. We agreed that I would talk with Steven (with his adoptive mother present) about my meeting with his birth mother. I would try to help him understand why things had gone wrong and to give him a fuller sense of his birth mother beyond his memories and his experience of her as a mother who had got things so terribly wrong.

A few days before my meeting date with Steven a package arrived through the post from his birth mother. Inside was a card as well as a bundle of swimming certificates and medals. After our meeting she had visited her own mother and asked if she had kept any of her old swimming awards. She had sent these to Steven with a message relaying her own love of swimming and her pride in his achievements. She had expressed a wish that Steven keep her own medals and a hope that he would understand that this represented a positive part of whom she had once been and perhaps a positive part of their identity that they could share. I discussed the package with Steven's adoptive parents and they felt it would be beneficial for him to receive it.

Talking to Steven about my meeting with his birth mother and passing on the package that she had sent for him with a highly emotive experience. Steven was incredibly sad when thinking about his birth mother's early life; he felt sadness for his birth mother but also for himself. His anger towards her did not magically evaporate; these were complex feelings that would take a lifetime to come to terms with. His increased understanding of his birth mother as an individual whose life had changed so drastically over time helped him to begin to think about her in a more rounded sense. His surprise and joy that they shared a positive connection was clear to see. Steven understood the value of the gift that she had given to him in wanting him to 'hold on to' the more positive sense of identity that she had once had in the child that she had once been.

* *

This is one example of how letterbox contact can help adopted teenagers to make sense of their birth family member's identity, and who they are, in a much wider sense. Sometimes young people ask much more simple questions: what television programmes do they like to watch, do they live in a nice place, what is their favourite food? In my experience, even these more day-to-day enquiries help the young person, as time goes by, to build an understanding of their birth parent or other birth relative, which is more widely defined than just the account of 'what went wrong'. It is a difficult balance for teenagers, and indeed for us as adults, to hold in mind the fact that as human beings we are much more complex than 'good' or 'bad', particularly when an individual's actions have caused so much harm. Yet, I do believe that using letterbox contact as an opportunity to begin to understand the fuller and more complex picture of the birth family member's identity and background is valuable. Adolescents are at a particular advantage in being able to undertake this exploration, as we have seen in previous chapters. If parents are alert to the questions, feelings and fantasies that young people may hold in relation to the contact exchange, contact can be a very useful opportunity to address some of those identity issues discussed earlier in the book and provide a voice in order to begin to articulate their exploration. Professionals need to be ready to support adoptive parents in making sense of the young person's feelings that come to the fore as a result of the letterbox contact and to be able to support birth parents in providing a response to the young person's questions. In my experience, many birth parents will be able to do this when the request for information comes as a direct result of the teenager's expressed needs. Finally, professionals will need to be ready to support the adoptive parents and the young person in making sense of the wider communication that results from these initial explorations.

The potential for letterbox contact to reassure the teenager about the birth family's wellbeing

Receiving regular letters from birth family members can play an important part in reassuring young people that they are safe and well. Teenagers do worry about their birth family's ongoing wellbeing after they have been removed from them; this is often particularly the case for young people who have experienced domestic violence or other experiences that have posed a very real threat to their birth family members' safety. If letterbox contact is possible, it can alleviate some of this anxiety.

In some situations it simply won't be possible to reassure the young person about their birth family member's welfare, because the birth family member is not OK. The effects of long-term drug and alcohol abuse, violence or just poor health in itself can mean that birth family members die. This may be a reality that many adopted teenagers have to come to terms with and is likely to be experienced with a new intensity in the adolescent years. In these situations, families will often require additional support to help the young person cope with yet further loss.

Contact from birth family members can reassure the adolescent that the family still thinks about and cares for them

I have worked with many birth parents who, with support, have managed to provide this message via contact in an appropriate and sensitive way. It is important because many teenagers will worry that their birth parent or other birth relative no longer cares for them or thinks about them once they have been adopted. Many adopted young people will struggle with feelings of rejection and abandonment because of their past experiences. Appropriate messages to the effect that birth family members still think about them, care for them and want them to be happy can help to alleviate the sense of rejection and abandonment that some young people carry with them. It is important to consider, however, the nature of the messages we are communicating to children from birth family members. Sometimes birth parents will be able to do this but when they are not, it can be possible to find this message communicated from another birth family member.

Taking responsibility and apologizing

If a birth parent is able to provide the message within contact that they take responsibility for not being able to care for the young person and apologize for this, it can be of enormous benefit. This book has highlighted the need for young people to make sense of their lives, what happened and why. If birth family members are able to help with this in acknowledging that things did go wrong, that it wasn't the young person's fault and that they are sorry that the young person suffered the adverse experiences they did, it is an incredibly healing process. This won't always be possible but if adoptive parents recognize that their child may be struggling with feelings of self-blame and confusion in regard to why they were removed from their birth family, it is worth seeking support from the post-adoption social work team that manages contact to see if this would be possible. Some parents who have maintained ongoing contact with birth family members over a long period of time may feel able to broach this issue with them directly.

Helping to process birth family history

Contact can also provide a trigger for discussing and processing the experience and meaning of birth family history for adopted young people. Young people do not often have the words to ask the questions that can help them to make sense of their experiences, nor indeed to be aware of the questions they may have. As we have seen in previous chapters, these gaps are likely to emerge in sometimes worrying and challenging behaviours. Teenagers who have a life-story book that was produced for them when they were five years old may struggle to make sense of their current, more sophisticated needs in relation to their history and identity with that tool alone. It can also be confusing in trying to make sense of things from an account of their history, which is effectively 'frozen in time'. Ongoing contact affords the opportunity for these narratives to become a more fluid and ongoing part of the young person's developing understanding and provides an awareness of birth family members also getting older and perhaps changing over time.

Important messages of support and acceptance from adoptive parents

When adoptive parents are able to facilitate contact in an open and reflective way for their children they are providing positive messages of acceptance and ability to 'hold' and process difficult feelings for them. Acknowledgement of the teenager's complex identity needs, acceptance of their different genetic inheritance and ability to help the young person think and feel about their past within the context of the different developmental stages (and particularly this one) are key tasks for adoptive parents. Helping the young person to engage in contact and providing a clear message that the adoptive parent is alongside them in supporting them with this is a very powerful way of communicating the above. They are also maintaining a sense of the past and present as being integrated for the young person. This will support teenagers, particularly, in not developing a sense of 'divided loyalty'.

Maintaining contact arrangements and supporting the young person in their needs within it is, of course, much more straightforward and less scary when it happens in an organized and moderated way. What, though, are the considerations when teenagers take contact into their own hands and either step outside of the boundaries of previous arrangements or, for those teenagers, who haven't had any contact arrangements, instigate initial contact with birth family members?

What may happen if the teenager makes 'new' contact with their birth family?

It is common for teenagers to start seeking 'unregulated' contact with birth family members outside of the constraints of previous contact arrangements once they move into adolescence because of the factors highlighted at the beginning of this chapter. While parents' influence on their children's decisions can feel diminished, earlier stages of positive contact can impact on the outcomes of teenagers' 'unregulated contact' in their adolescent years.

. . . . OLIVIA AGED 14 . . . .

I worked with a teenage girl, Olivia, who at 14 years of age had made contact with birth family members via Facebook. Fortunately, her adoptive parents had been having regular letterbox contact with

Olivia's birth mother and grandmother from the time of Olivia's placement with them. The relationship between the adults had developed in time and there was a sense of trust and understanding between both the birth and adoptive family that Olivia's wellbeing mattered to each of them. Their conversation about Olivia had been an ongoing one for 11 years.

Although Olivia's adoptive parents felt that it was too soon for Olivia to be having direct contact with her birth family, they knew that Olivia did not share this view. They worried that she would travel to her birth family without them unless they were proactive in thinking about managing Olivia's need for direct contact at that stage. Consequently, they arranged a meeting with Olivia's birth mother and grandmother and suggested that they all meet together with Olivia to give her the opportunity to see her mother and grandmother, but with a strong message that they and the birth family members were thinking about her needs.

The meeting went well and they agreed that they would meet regularly together in the future. Olivia, however, was entering a period in her life in which she was struggling with her identity, and, indeed, in individuating in a secure way. She struggled with school and her peer relationships and began to rebel, staying away from home and expressing a high degree of rejection towards her adoptive parents. Inevitably, one day she 'ran away' and arrived unannounced at her birth mother's home address. In a panic and not knowing what to do for Olivia, her birth mother phoned her adoptive mother and let her know that she was there. This was a very powerful message for Olivia; her birth mother was working with her adoptive mother in trying to respond appropriately to her. The nature of the relationship between the adoptive and birth families had to adjust yet again in meeting Olivia's needs.

There followed a period of time in which the contact between the birth and adoptive family took on a completely new shape. Olivia herself was given the opportunity to undertake some therapeutic work and eventually she began to feel more 'at ease' with her identity and unresolved feelings of anger and loss. This was not a path that either the adoptive or birth family would ever have imagined when they began letterbox contact when she was three years of age. I have no doubt that without their shared history of letterbox contact they would not have been able to adapt together to Olivia's changing needs in the way they did. Their ability to be flexible and pragmatic in their approach was very much to Olivia's benefit during that difficult period of her life.

. . . .

When there haven't been any previous arrangements, and adoptive parents are unable to draw on an ongoing relationship with birth parents, this can be much trickier. Parents are unlikely to know what the current situation is within the birth family, what the birth family's views are about the adoption and what their intentions and needs are in regard to the contact.

Building in safety for teenagers who are searching

Whilst it may be very challenging for parents to take an open and accepting stance to the teenager's emotional need to instigate new contact arrangements with birth family members, it is incredibly important to try and do so. Attempting to 'shut down' the young person's need is unlikely to be effective and more likely to push the teenager into more secretive behaviour. If parents can try and take important elements of the PACE approach in addressing this issue, they are more likely to be able to have influence on the way in which the young person behaves in relation to contact. Helping the young person to identify the emotional need in wanting to have contact, consider what the positive and negative outcomes of it may be and be realistic about expectations will be important in supporting them. Issues around safety will be a key consideration. Teenagers are likely to minimize any risks but parents need to hold these in mind for them. If parents are involved in the young person's thinking processes and plans in regard to contact they may be able to 'build in' safety buffers that the young person hasn't considered. If a parent realizes that the young person is likely to meet with birth family members even if there is parental and professional advice to the contrary, they may be able to suggest that this happens in a safe venue, for example. Parents can also support the young person safely by being a part of the contact or (if the young person is struggling with this) by enlisting the support of another family member or even a social worker from the post-adoption team. Social services (particularly the post-adoption teams) may also be able to help in finding out information about the birth family's current circumstances and even supporting birth family members in managing the contact. If the approach is a flexible and considered one, the parents are more likely to be able to be alongside the young person in any contact they may make. Unfortunately, there are sometimes birth family members who may pose a very real physical risk to the young person. In these cases it is important to inform your post-adoption team of your concerns so that they can help to manage the situation.

It may be necessary to seek therapeutic support in approaching the contact issue in teenage years. Parents may need their own therapeutic support, as they may experience strong feelings of rejection and fear in relation to the young person's need to make contact with birth family members. The teenager is almost always likely to benefit from support that will help to place their needs in regard to contact within a wider context. Life-story work is likely to be particularly beneficial at this stage.

Therapeutic support may also provide the opportunity for contact to take place in a facilitated way. Facilitated contact is a planned contact meeting in which all parties are supported in meeting together and prepared for particular questions the teenager may have. This can be extremely useful in reducing anxiety and structuring initial meetings and can also ensure that the young person's needs are central to the contact.

Do they have to go there to come back?

When teenagers take contact into their own hands and seek this out before they are 18 it can be a very worrying time for adoptive parents. Many of the young people I have worked with have needed to do this and go through this process as a part of understanding who they are and resolving their feelings about the past. My experience is that they may sometimes oscillate between adoptive and birth family identification as they figure things out in contact; sometimes they need to understand the reality of their birth family for themselves through this experience before they can feel more settled. There will be different outcomes for different young people in how they experience their birth family, and adoptive parents will often need to hang on in there as the young person goes through it. My strongest advice for parents, though, is to maintain communication wherever possible, to continue to provide a safe harbour for the young person and to be prepared to support the teenager in the difficulties they will inevitably encounter during this process. Teenagers are likely to have far more complex feelings in relation to contact than they will admit to in the early stages and will need their parents' emotional support.

Conclusion

I will end this chapter with observations and advice from parents who have experienced their teenager's exploration of contact with birth family members. The statements below illustrate many of the themes discussed within this chapter.

On worries about loss

I worried that 'blood is thicker than water' and we would stop being important to him from that point on.

On feeling out of control and seeking professional support

They all came via Facebook, birth parents, brothers, god knows who else. It felt out of control. He didn't know the gory details of what had happened in the past so he couldn't understand our panic. We had to ask social services for help. He needed to hear the details of his past from someone other than us because he thought we were just being awkward I think, trying to ruin it.

On feeling resigned

In the end I thought, well she has to do this for herself, I hoped that the reality of contact would place the birth family in perspective for her. It did, but I wish it had happened later because she was emotionally immature and unable to cope with the feelings it brought up.

I thought, alright, let's go with it and I'll pick up the pieces afterwards.

On witnessing the young person being hurt

It was so painful to watch him go through it. He rallied and ranted about her, how she was trash and a druggie and a liar and a bitch. I was scared of the degree of his rage when she rejected him like that but I knew that underneath he was in so much pain. He was desperate to be accepted by her, to have her say that she'd always loved him, to be a mum to him. His grief was palpable. I was so worried about him. How do you explain someone like that to a 17-year-old?

On using support to maintain the parent's resilience

I had to be fairly resilient to accept B's feelings for her birth mother, even though I felt anger at what B had been exposed to in her early years. These contacts were always difficult for me but fortunately with great support from social services they were manageable.

On being alongside the young person

We took the approach right from the beginning that we would rather be alongside her if she really wanted to do it. There were increased signs of curiosity right from the beginning of secondary school. We found her googling her birth mother's name. We were worried for her; there was this really profound fear that she was opening a Pandora's box that she couldn't handle. We were realistic though; we knew she was going to do it anyway. We thought we could probably offer a 'safe base' for her to return to, particularly when she started having direct contact with them. I think it was the right thing to do. She definitely went through a stage where she idealized them but gradually she witnessed more and more and I saw her turn away from them. It felt like she had to go there to come back.

On being open in expectations

Don't assume it will be disastrous. We actually met with the birth family before she did. The post-adoption social worker put in a lot of work to support them and us. They didn't hold any anger towards us. They could see that we had cared for her and that her life had been a positive one. They still had really significant problems but cared for her. One day she 'ran away' to go to their house after a row with us. Her older brother who was in his thirties by then called us and said that he would bring her back and gave her a talking to. I think that our acceptance that they remained a part of her gave them a lot of reassurance. There was no tug of war.

On managing the parent's feelings

My advice would be to try and put aside your fears of rejection, of them going back. I made a very conscious effort to say, 'Look I know you need to do this but I'm still here when you need me.' I bit my tongue (a lot), he had to go through it really. It's caused him more harm but there was no way of avoiding it. He's still here though, still with us and hopefully he'll get through this stage.

On communicating with the young person about birth family

Be open with your child [about the birth family] from the beginning but without judgement. Don't give reassurance that 'they love you' without explaining the context of that. In the end if your child has contact with them they might experience rejection again and again or get very hurt by 'a love' that exists within a relationship that will continue to be emotionally harmful.

PARENTS COME FIRST

The Importance of Support for Parents

Previous chapters have highlighted that parenting adolescents is a challenging task in itself and, importantly, that parenting adopted adolescents is particularly challenging.

This chapter will address the absolutely crucial issue of support for parents who are parenting adopted teenagers. Earlier chapters have, I hope, illustrated the fact that these parents face extremely complex and stressful challenges in meeting their children's needs during this developmental stage. This chapter will explore the impact on parents' wellbeing in more detail. Parents' individual experiences and views will be discussed and I will argue that it is simply not possible to expect parents to manage these complex and distressing situations without support. At present, this support is largely inadequate. Often, services (where they exist at all) focus on the child's needs without giving consideration to the reality that it is the parents who are carrying and managing the emotional distress of their children on a daily basis. Services struggle to meet the needs of these young people, yet parents are expected to meet them without sufficient support. As I have discussed, adopted adolescents have developmental needs that are 'above and beyond' those of their peers who have not experienced loss and trauma within their early lives. Their parents are providing parenting that is in excess of what their 'parent peers' are having to provide. Adoptive parents are their young people's protectors, their advocates and the people who absorb their trauma, fight for services, navigate the education possibilities, manage issues of contact, manage difficulties with peers and romantic relationships and sit in the police station, the court room, outside the therapy room and at home understanding that their young person is as yet ill prepared to be 'out in the world' but knowing that they cannot stop the developmental process that compels them to venture out before they are emotionally ready. They do this within the context of often shaky and fragile attachment relationships, which can be fraught with difficulty. They are often the only adults in the young person's life who are and will remain available as he or she moves into early adulthood and beyond. Without them, the teenager would be without anchor and yet they receive a woeful lack of support.

In 'I hate you get _____ but first take me and Alex into town.' Tony Wolf and Suzanne Franks explore what it is to be the parent of a teenager.

> What is it to be the parent of a teenager? It is to do what you think best – when really you have no idea what is best. It is to ride out the storms and be back again the next day. It is to continue to give love to a child who does not seem to want it, to a child who, five minutes earlier, seemed to deserve a slap more than anything else.[1]

This description will resonate with the majority of parents of adolescents but particularly with adoptive parents, who are doing all of the above but with additional complexities and subsequent stresses. It is important to recognize too that for many parents at this stage of parenting the stresses involved in the parenting relationship will not be the only challenges they are dealing with at this stage of life. Other stresses including responding to the needs of ageing parents, work-related difficulties, financial challenges, relationship difficulties, health issues and so on will inevitably be a feature of life at this time. It is important to recognize therefore that the stress of parenting is often taking place within the context of other challenges that can impact on the resilience of parents within their parenting role. Understanding this only emphasizes further the need for sufficient support.

Parent-focused support: what are the difficulties and what support may be helpful?
A lack of understanding from family and friends
Many parents whose children have additional needs resulting from their early experiences find that their family and friend networks are unable to understand the nature of these needs. This lack of understanding can often, in turn, lead to a lack of understanding of the parenting choices that adoptive parents have to make.

> I want to scream at those people who have passed judgement on me 'She wasn't firm enough' or 'How about sports?', like I haven't tried both.

> I wasn't prepared for the difficulty my extended family would have with some of the behaviour of my son resulting from his early trauma. Now he is a teenager I can't take my son to see my mum, she is so shocked by the reality of his difficult eating habits – she thinks it's bad parenting. So family occasions can be tense and need to be planned for. They were very happy for us when he arrived but haven't been able to absorb the facts about attachment and early trauma and the effects on behaviour as he gets get older.

It is incredibly difficult for family and friends to support parents sufficiently if they don't understand that they are having to adjust their parenting to the particular needs of their child. The child's needs aren't easily understood and there is often no 'diagnostic label' that helps to 'evidence' that these difficulties are real. Family and friends may struggle to understand that the young person's struggles are a case of 'can't do' rather than 'won't do' and that parents are having to parent in a counterintuitive way because the 'usual' parenting techniques are not effective. This lack of understanding can lead to parents feeling judged by those from whom they would seek support and also very isolated.

The solutions

A way of tackling this difficulty would be to provide 'family-and-friend' network meetings about the impact of trauma and loss on young people's development so that parents' support networks could understand both the nature of the difficulties that the young person experiences and the implications for parenting approaches. These meetings could provide psycho-education elements as well as helping friends and family members understand the impact on parents (and themselves in supporting the parents and young person). The meetings could also provide an opportunity for those attending to think about useful support that they could provide and what they would need in order to provide this and to explore how the network could combine resources so that the parents would feel sufficiently supported. I would suggest that whilst it would be extremely helpful to have these meetings at regular intervals throughout adolescence (particularly when parents are in crisis), it would also be very helpful if they could take place at key points in the young person's development throughout their earlier childhood. Some voluntary adoption agencies and local authorities do undertake these meetings around the time of the child's initial placement, but meetings at key developmental stages such as mid-childhood would be very useful in maintaining a discussion and support around the family so that this process is established prior to adolescence.

Another area of provision that could be useful in helping those around the family to support parents and their children is training. The majority of local authorities run a range of parenting-support based training for adoptive parents. Having the provision for parents to take a key supportive figure to these training sessions, or indeed to run family-and-friends training or workshop days, would enhance the ability of those in the family's support network to be alongside parents in their task. Training about the particular challenges of adolescence would, of course, be particularly valuable, for friends-and-family networks.

It is, though, the case that despite the best intentions, it may be difficult for family and friends to comprehend fully the quality of parents' experiences, as these can be so removed from others' experiences of parenting. The value of shared experience with those who 'truly get it' cannot be underestimated.

> Finding a network of supportive relationships for parents seems crucial in giving us the reflective space to move through adolescence.[2]

There are resources in place for adoptive parents to share their experiences and seek advice from other adoptive parents in a similar position. Adoption UK provides these services, which have always been well received by adoptive parents. A group called Parents of Traumatised Adopted Teens Organisation (POTATO) has also been identified by parents as being very supportive. It describes its services as follows:

We are a UK based group of parents who have adopted our children from the looked after system in the past 20 years. All of our teenagers are incredible survivors who need specialist parenting which can be very hard going. Despite dealing with some heavy subjects, we like to meet socially and have a bit of relaxation with other parents who understand what we are facing.

The group also develops programmes and resources for parents as well as providing an online support forum and campaigning for change in key areas of policy and support.

Another valuable resource for adoptive parents can be a facilitated and ongoing group for parents, which meets regularly and on a long-term basis. I have been running a group in North London for the past three years with two colleagues from the local authority post-adoption teams. The group has been very successful in meeting this area of need and receives ongoing funding from the North London Adoption and Fostering Consortium. One of the overarching aims of the project was to provide a forum in which parents could gain support from other parents who were experiencing similar difficulties to their own. In bringing parents together, it was hoped that their experiences would be 'normalized' for them, reducing some of the feelings of blame and shame that they had been subjected to and indeed had internalized because of their experiences.

The aim of the content of the group sessions was to provide theoretical perspectives (as highlighted throughout this book) that would help the parents to understand why their children struggled in key areas.

The sessions follow a semi-structured format exploring key areas of concern. The areas of concern were clarified in partnership with the parents attending the group at the beginning of the project and include the key themes discussed in earlier chapters. The practical implications of these areas are explored in relation to the parents' individual experiences within group exercises and discussion.

The themes are explored from the perspective of the teenagers' emotional experiences whilst retaining a focus on the emotional impact of the challenges in these areas on the parents themselves. The feedback from this group has been overwhelmingly positive with respondents identifying improvements in the areas identified in relation to both the overarching aims of the group and the aims within the content of the sessions. In commenting on the value of group support provision parents have stated that:

> To know other parents with teenagers are going through similar experiences has been absolutely invaluable.

> It has been brilliant listening to the experiences of others and talking through my own experiences. It is so helpful to understand the common threads and recognize the difficult behaviour and that it is a result of our children's early experiences.

> A very supportive and safe environment has been created by the trainer. It is really helpful for me to meet with other parents and share experiences in a way where we are also thinking positively about what we can do differently rather than despairing.

Members also felt very strongly that using theoretical perspectives to underpin the content of the sessions had increased their understanding of their children's inner emotional worlds. This understanding had positively impacted on their relationship with their children:

> This group has been an incredible lifeline for me in recent months. It has provided me with insight and explanations to better understand and support my child and our relationship.

The insight and understanding I have gained from participating in the group has been priceless to me and my relationship with my child.

Parents were also clear, however, that the focus on practical strategies within the group content had been of particular value for them:

Each session has managed to give me concrete tips and useful phrases and thoughts to share with my daughter. It has also given me valuable time to reflect and think about our time together.

I listen to my child more. I have some understanding of her own unique situation, while not 'pathologizing' her experiences. I have been 'humbled' by the knowledge and understanding of my child's emotional/psychological survival skills!

Too often I go to courses and we look at the problems and we hear about some of the explanations but never get to the 'so how do we deal with this/help our children'. This course is different and I would happily go on coming to it for years.

The primary value of the group has been in bringing parents together; it is my strong belief that this provision would be valuable in all areas of the country.

A lack of understanding from professionals

The distress of parenting traumatized young people is compounded for parents when they both struggle to find effective support and, in the process of seeking support, receive negative and punitive responses from professionals. There are, of course, many positive service provisions. Some of the adoptive parents I have worked with have received excellent support from well-informed and skilled local authority post-adoption teams and from CAMHS. In my experience, parents are also generally very positive about the services they receive from specialist adoption-focused agencies. One of the primary difficulties is the inconsistent nature of support throughout the country. Unfortunately, many adoptive parents will struggle to be directed towards the right support (even when it is available). The nature of the difficulties they are dealing with and their distressed presentation may then also be interpreted in a way that causes them further distress.

Adopters had often rung Children's Services for help and had been directed to the children and families team rather than the post-adoption services. It was difficult to know whether the adopters' tone of voice, their desperation, or the way they spoke about the child had triggered social workers' concerns. It would not be surprising if parents in their distressed state had sounded angry or cold. Many were worn down, worn out, and frightened. It might also have been possible that children's social workers would view the cause of children's challenging behavior, as neglectful or inadequate parenting. Although all the parents refuted these accusations, a few did state that on occasions they had responded aggressively, been critical and had lacked warmth. Parents described how they struggled to convince social workers that their parenting capacity had been compromised by the difficulties they had been experiencing often for many years and not that their child's difficulties had emerged, as a consequence of their poor parenting.[3]

It is a devastating experience to seek help and then be treated as though it is you who is responsible for your child's difficulties. To have the threat of your child being removed, to find yourself the subject of child protection processes.

A lack of knowledge and understanding about the impact of early trauma and loss and the lifelong implications of them are often at the root of social workers' less helpful responses to adoptive parents. Responses to families when the difficulties seem to be so complex and difficult to resolve can also be influenced by a sense of helplessness and frustration that leaves professionals unable to 'hold' the difficulties and painful feelings effectively. Services can become blaming and punitive. Splitting is always a risk when professionals and agencies are working with highly traumatized children. Often professionals will find themselves taking opposing positions in relation to both parents and services or indeed to the adolescents they are working with.

> Unable to hold painful and conflicting feelings can lead to 'fault lines' in provision to families with services failing to meet needs and moving into despairing, punitive and ultimately ineffective attempts as supporting families.[4]

Adoption in itself also often carries particular expectations and hopes that other long-term care arrangements don't. There can be very strong belief systems among professionals that a loving family is the 'cure all' for children who have had very difficult early experiences. Much is invested in the need to rescue children and 'make things better'; adoptive parents can find themselves holding the disappointment, confusion and thwarted hopes of others when this doesn't happen.

Professional systems can also struggle to hold and meet the level of risk that teenagers can present with. It has often struck me that we are asking parents to hold risk, make difficult decisions and balance conflicting needs, but we struggle to do this as professionals within our existing systems.

Solutions in providing improved professional responses

It is incredibly important that any referrals to services concerning adopted adolescents are directed to or co-worked with well-informed post-adoption teams, who can help other teams to understand the particular context of the factors that will have contributed to the family's experience. I do believe that it would be beneficial for services to have written guidelines and procedures when responding to child protection referrals involving young people in permanent care arrangements. The need to understand the relationship between children's earlier traumas and child protection concerns that may arise in the present is crucial if services are to provide well-informed and sound assessments. Post-adoption teams themselves benefit from ongoing training in relation to the impact of trauma and loss and child development generally and should have access to consultation from similarly informed psychological services that can help workers to assess needs effectively but also process the very challenging feelings that can arise when involved with families.

We have to remember as professionals that adoptive parents began their journey with a sincere motivation to become parents, to have a family and, often, to provide a home for children who had endured extremely stressful and traumatic early lives. The presentation of those very same parents, experiencing a crisis in their child's adolescence, may well be of parents in a state of flight, fight or freeze. It is crucial that, in supporting these parents, services understand the impact of living with trauma and the debilitating impact of this on parenting capacity. If we begin with this understanding, we can work on the premise that with sufficient support these parents can return to a healthier emotional state with an increased capacity to meet their child's complex needs. If we don't hold this in mind, we risk moving into punitive and damaging approaches to the very people who offer the best chance of recovery for their children. We cannot, of course, discount the possibility that young people can be abused within any family context, but beginning any assessment with an open mind and a secure, knowledge-based approach is absolutely essential if we are to avoid unnecessarily adding to families' distress and the risk of disruption.

A particular note about the impact of violence

In my experience of working with adoptive parents, a very high proportion of them will have experienced aggressive behaviour from the young person. This aggressive behaviour is often physical. Julie Selwyn's research highlights this as a key factor in disruptions.[5] 'Child-to-parent (and child-to-sibling) violence was the main reason young people had had to leave home in permanent care arrangements. Parents lived in fear and gave many examples of being beaten, suddenly attacked, threatened, intimidated and controlled. The impact on parents' emotional health of enduring physical attacks is profound. Parents describe feeling frightened, impotent, overwhelmed, helpless, angry, isolated and ashamed in response to these experiences. Maintaining a positive relationship with the young person in the face of these attacks is understandably extremely difficult. Services often responded to these difficulties with an assumption that the responsibility for the violence must lie in the parents' inadequate or even abusive parenting.

Solutions for managing violence

Stopping aggressive behaviour, be it verbal or physical, is not easy and it is important for parents to seek therapeutic support for both the young person and themselves if this is happening. Therapeutic support will not, necessarily, achieve quick results though, and it is therefore important in the meantime that parents take care of their own physical safety and the young person as far as possible. In discussing this issue with a group of parents who had all experienced aggression from their young people, they highlighted the following as important factors to have in place.

- Don't keep instances of physical violence a secret. Let those adults who are close to you know and let your child know that they know. Be clear that you are doing this because you and your child need to be safe and you need others to be able to support you. This sends a clear message that the problem is one that cannot remain 'a secret', that it is too serious to manage just within the home.

- If possible, use supportive figures within the family-and-friends network who can talk with the young person and provide respite if needed. Messages about the unacceptability and seriousness of violence need to come from as many safe adults within the network as possible. This message needs to be delivered with empathy and understanding of the young person's difficulties, but also with a clear message that it cannot continue without being addressed because both their and the parents' safety are paramount.

- Have a 'safety plan' worked out. If physical violence occurs, alert a friend or neighbour (who is aware of the difficulties) so that they come round to the home to support you if necessary.

- If you are very concerned for your safety and there is a pattern of violence, involve the police. Many parents worry about getting their child into further trouble, but allowing violence to continue unchecked can risk physical safety. The young person also needs a clear message that violent behaviour is society's concern, not just the family's. Most parents spoke very highly of the police's response and some parents had a very positive experience of speaking to a local police representative to explain the circumstances before instances occurred so that the police response could be as well informed as possible.

- Address what has happened when violent incidents have occurred *when the situation is calmer*; emphasize the importance of safety and understand that the young person won't feel safe when they are out of control either. If possible, try to establish particular triggers to anger and work out a way of managing the situation before it escalates into violence. The young person may have their own ideas about this that they can contribute. It may, however, be the case that this is only possible with therapeutic support and it may be a complex process.

There is an increasing awareness of the severity of child-to-parent violence within services and courses such as 'non violent resistance' can also provide support for parents and families in this area. The strategies suggested by parents in managing violence within the home are reflected in these programmes.[6] A sea change in professional understanding of the complexities of the causes driving violent behaviour, as well as an informed and prompt response that doesn't begin with a blaming stance, will be one that is very much welcomed by parents.

The real impact of secondary trauma and the reality of the presence of primary trauma for adoptive parents

Secondary trauma is often discussed as a phenomenon that occurs for people who have the responsibility for caring for someone who has been through a crisis. The Child Trauma Academy website (www.childtrauma.com) discusses the potential for professionals working with traumatized children in developing secondary trauma. It argues that those caring for traumatized children are at increased risk of developing secondary trauma for a number of reasons. Because those caring for traumatized children are empathizing with the child, they are vulnerable to internalizing the child's trauma-related pain. Often there is insufficient recovery time in between hearing about the young person's trauma before being exposed to this again. Professionals may have their own unresolved personal trauma that may be reactivated by the young person's experiences. Professionals are often working within systemic fragmentation and isolation; the impact of this is that they are experiencing higher levels of stress because they are not adequately supported by cohesive teams that can help to regulate their stress reactions. They are often working with a lack of systemic resources, which causes additional levels of stress. Whilst these factors are discussed within the context of the workplace I would argue that secondary trauma is a particular risk for adoptive parents because of the very same factors. Kate Cairns has undertaken some important work in this area and her book *Attachment, Trauma and Resilience: Therapeutic Caring for Children* (2002) is a very useful resource.[7] Many adoptive parents are internalizing their child's emotional pain, have very little recovery time, have their own experiences of unresolved trauma, are isolated and have insufficient support. Some of the symptoms of secondary trauma are feelings of anger and sadness, prolonged grief, anxiety and depression. Physical indicators can include headaches, stomach aches, lethargy and constipation. Personal indicators can include self-isolation, cynicism, mood swings and irritability with the spouse and family. Many adoptive parents will experience some or all of these symptoms at different stages in their child's development.[8]

Sadly, even when circumstances may be calmer, parents are often left in a state of high alert, their own stress responses at a permanently high pitch. An adoptive father I worked with described his hyper vigilance to further crisis:

Even if I was sat reading the paper I'd be waiting for the next call, like being a fireman sat in the station waiting for the alarm to go and being on high alert to jump up and fire fight.

The impact of this chronic stress on parents' physical and emotional health can be very serious. It is, of course, misleading to talk only in terms of secondary trauma, many parents will be living not just with this, but also with the primary trauma of concerning instances in the present too.

Solutions for managing the impact of stress for parents

The provision of therapeutic support for parents is absolutely crucial. I have often found that services focus the provision of this support on the young person, with parents offered either a limited amount of provision as an addition to the primary work or none at all. As the young person's primary support, the parents need to be supported in equal measure if they are to provide containment and safety. When we consider the nature of the stress that many parents are under, it is unrealistic to expect them to support the young person within their process unless they have the opportunity for reflection and the space to have their own emotional needs met. At the very least, parents should receive specific parent support sessions that provide both containment for those feelings and help in understanding what is going on for the young person. A focus on useful parenting approaches and specific strategies for managing behaviours can be very valuable for parents. The approach to this work should always be collaborative, with the worker taking a position 'alongside' parents if they are to feel both supported and empowered in their parenting role. Whenever possible, parents should be involved in the therapeutic work with the young person in order that they can support him or her effectively within and outside of the therapeutic sessions. It is also important to hold in mind the degree of strain that parenting young people with the kind of difficulties discussed can take on couple relationships. Parents may often find themselves in conflict with one another as they struggle to meet the adolescent's needs and this can compound the stress experienced for each individual parent still further. Supporting couples in their own relationship is often an important part of this work and sufficient time needs to be given to this.

Self-care is very important for parents who are under a great deal of strain. Parents I have worked with have acknowledged that it can be difficult to find the time (or indeed give themselves permission to have the time) to take care of themselves. The value of undertaking activities that help to relax and take the parent away from the stress of the relationship cannot be overstated. Walking, swimming, spending time with friends or (particularly) 'right-brained' activities, such as painting, singing and so on, are vital in giving the brain 'a break' from stress. Taking time out from the situation may sometimes seem a luxury or too much of an effort, but it helps to maintain resilience and good emotional health for parents. Other resources can also be helpful. Adoptionplus offers parents mindfulness provision in the recognition that this can help parents in their resilience. Patricia Downing, counsellor and mindfulness practitioner describes this below.

> Mindfulness is increasingly seen as a useful resource for parents, and particularly helpful for highly stressful parenting relationships. Mindfulness is defined as 'paying attention in a particular way: on purpose, in the present moment, and non-judgementally' (Kabat-Zinn 1994).[9] This means cultivating a greater awareness of our moment-to-moment experience, both in terms of physical sensations in the body and the thought processes of our minds. When we bring awareness to sensations in the body, we direct the mind away from thinking and in the process activate different areas of the brain. This can be useful if our thoughts are building a

story about a situation, perhaps judging it as 'too hard' or 'impossible' for example, which in turn can make us feel helpless or angry. If we are able mentally to step back from the situation briefly, we may be less likely to react and risk exacerbating an already volatile situation. Research shows that levels of the stress hormone, cortisol, are lowered when people do regular mindfulness meditation, indicating the potential for physiological change.

The stress of parenting an adopted teenager may mean that it is very difficult to hold on to clear thinking, in the face of perhaps chaotic and aggressive behavior. Ways of helping yourself stay as calm as possible in the face of such challenges are important. Mindfulness can also enable us to regain a calmer state if, on occasion, we become angry or upset by what is happening. After all, we are human and not perfect, so we will not always manage to act in the way we would wish to. A key aspect of mindfulness is compassion, towards ourselves as well as to others.

An ideal way to learn more about mindfulness is to attend an 8 week MBSR (Mindfulness Based Stress Reduction) or MBCT (Mindfulness Based Cognitive Therapy) course. There are also courses and resources online (see www. mindfulnessteachersuk.org.uk), plus some excellent books such as *Mindfulness: Finding Peace in a Frantic World* by Mark Williams and Danny Penman. There are also CDs with mindfulness practices, to get started. It is important to identify a mindfulness practitioner who is trained to run mindfulness courses, who meets the recommended guidelines (see www. mindfulnessteachersuk.org.uk for more information) and is using mindfulness approaches in their own daily life, when looking for a course or group in your local area.

There is increasing evidence emerging on the benefits of mindfulness, for lowering stress levels, improving relationships, optimizing physical health, improving emotional intelligence, reducing anxiety and being helpful in depression. It has also been shown to improve brain function, increasing grey matter in areas associated with self-awareness, empathy, self-control and attention.

Self-care in reflecting on your own experiences

Chapter Three highlighted the importance for parents of taking care of their own emotional health in parenting effectively. Mindfulness may be one of the strategies in managing stress but more focused attention to the impact of past and present vulnerabilities for parents and the risks of these to 'blocked care' may be required. Useful strategies for self-reflection are available in approaches such as Dan Seigel's *The Wheel of Awareness*[10] but some parents may need the professional support available from a psychotherapist or counsellor.

Conclusion

In concluding this chapter, I turn again to the observations made by parents and some of their suggestions in regard to the type and value of support important to them in managing their often challenging roles.

On messages to service provision

Make sure you are a resource for parents. Believe that they are doing their very best but need real support and be ready to put that in place.

A message to policy makers – somehow there needs to be a more straightforward path to the right post-adoption support for as long as is needed and that may be a long time.

Support from professionals who really understand and know how to try and help has been crucial for me.

On accessing effective support

Taking the decision to plug into as much support as possible but importantly also hooking up with the professionals who are highly experienced in this field (and ditching the ones who just don't get it) has been the best thing I've done.

It was such a relief to be understood.

On the value of contact with other adopters

Other adoptive parents have been the best support – realizing that our children have something in common and that the experiences of the very first few months are the main determinants of their difficult behaviour.

On the potential value of being prepared

It would be very helpful to know about potential issues before we get to the crisis; to know what might come up and why.

On the value of supportive partners and wider family

Having my partner to help me cope with some of the most horrendous and stressful situations I have ever experienced. He has actively taken over when I couldn't 'do it' any more. I wouldn't have survived this without him.

On the value of friends

At difficult times I would hide in the bedroom or bathroom and call one of my friends, just sharing the feelings helped to decrease my anxiety.

Supporting parents has a direct impact on the adopted teenager's wellbeing; when working with young people it is my experience that they feel safer when they know their parents are receiving support, this is a very powerful and containing message to young people. Parents need to receive our empathy and understanding in just the same way that we provide this for the young people we work with.

CONCLUSION

This book has focused on the challenges that can arise for adopted teenagers and their parents, because the aim of the book was to provide some exploration of approaches that may be helpful in addressing those challenges.

It is important to say, though, that the difficulties encountered by adopted teenagers and their parents are not the whole story. All of the parents I have worked with love their children and do the best they can for them under often very challenging circumstances. It is this love and dedication that makes such an important difference to the young people we have been discussing. Love, persistence, resilience and an ongoing ability to find joy and appreciate the small successes for their teenagers are what ultimately make the difference for their adopted child. I haven't yet met a teenager I've worked with who hasn't been able to acknowledge the vital role that their adoptive parents play in their lives. Whilst they often don't communicate this well to their parents(!), teenagers' understanding of the impact of their parents' love is clear within their reflections in therapeutic work.

Parenting is the most powerful tool we have in making a difference to the lives of the children who have been through extremely difficult times in their early years. Whilst the road can get particularly rocky during adolescence, the ability of parents to persevere does make a difference to the way in which the young person emerges 'out of the other side' into early adulthood.

The complexities of this group of young people do, though, demand that we don't 'leave parents to it'. We owe them our support; they are in need of services that: are adoption-focused; understand the needs of teenagers who have been affected by early experiences of trauma and loss; are able to work effectively with adolescents and their parents together. These services need to be available until the 'end' of adolescence at 25 years.

If we are able to meet the emotional challenges for these young people as they progress through adolescence, they will have every opportunity to emerge as young adults who can embark on a life that is fulfilling and rewarding, with the potential to develop healthy and secure relationships and, perhaps, to one day become attuned, loving and successful parents themselves. Sometimes it is the struggles we face that help us to become who we are in fulfilling our potential, rather than being left stuck in the trauma of the past.

REFERENCES

Introduction

1   Selwyn, J., Wijedasa, D. and Meakings, S. (2014) *Beyond the Adoption Order: Challenges, Interventions and Adoption Disruption*. Research report. Bristol: University of Bristol School for Policy Studies, Hadley Centre for Adoption and Foster Care Studies.
2   Selwyn, J., Wijedasa, D. and Meakings, S. (2014) p.146.
3   Selwyn, J., Wijedasa, D. and Meakings, S. (2014) p.147.
4   Selwyn, J., Wijedasa, D. and Meakings, S. (2014) p.148.
5   Selwyn, J., Wijedasa, D. and Meakings, S. (2014) p.148.
6   Price, E. and Sydney, L. (2014) *Facilitating Meaningful Contact in Adoption and Fostering*. London: Jessica Kingsley Publishers. pp.21–24.
7   Kaniuk, J., Steele, M. and Hodges, J. (2004) 'Report on a longitudinal research project, exploring the development of attachments between older, hard-to-place children and their adopters over the first two years of placement.' *Adoption and Fostering 28*, 2, 61–67.
8   Hughes, D. and Baylin, J. (2012) *Brain-Based Parenting: The Neuroscience of Caregiving for Healthy Attachment*. New York: W.W. Norton & Company. p.30.
9   Siegel, D. J. (2014) *Brainstorm*. Australia: Scribe.
10 Siegel, D. J. (2014) p.7.
11 Siegel, D. J. (2014) p.8.
12 Siegel, D. J. (2014) p.8.

13 Siegel, D. J. (2014) p.8.
14 Siegel, D. J. (2014) p.8.
15 Siegel, D. J. (2014) p.98.
16 Siegel, D. J. (2014) p.97.
17 Siegel, D. J. (2014) p.90.
18 Sunderland, M. (ed.) (2012) *Helping Teenagers with Anger and Low Self-Esteem.* Buckingham: Hinton House. p.108.
19 Siegel, D. J. (2014) p.149.
20 Siegel, D. J. (2014) p.145.
21 Bomber, L. M. (2011) *What About Me? Inclusive Strategies to Support Pupils with Attachment Difficulties Make it Through the School Day.* London: Worth Publishing.

Chapter One

1 Siegel, D. J. (2014) p.8.
2 Siegel, D. J. (2014) p.103.
3 Keck, G. C. (2009) *Parenting Adopted Adolescents: Understanding and Appreciating their Journeys.* Colorado Springs, CO: NavPress. p.55.
4 Brodinsky, D. M., Schechter, M. D. and Marantz Henig, R. (1993) *Being Adopted, the Lifelong Search for Self.* New York: Anchor Books. p.18.
5 Verrier, N. (1993) *The Primal Wound.* Baltimore, MD: Gateway Press.
6 Music, G. (2011) *Nurturing Natures.* Hove: Psychology Press. p.190.
7 Music, G. (2011) p.194.
8 Music, G. (2011) p.188.
9 Keck, G. C. (2009) p.33.
10 Sunderland, M. (2003) *Helping Children Locked in Rage or Hate.* Brackley: Speechmark. p. 3.
11 Golding, K. S. (2008) *Nurturing Attachments: Supporting Children who are Fostered or Adopted.* London: Jessica Kingsley Publishers. p.163.
12 Taransaud, D. (2011) *You Think I'm Evil.* London: Worth Publishing. p.31.
13 Sunderland, M. (2012) p.113.
14 Taransaud, D. (2011).

15   Taransaud, D. (2011) p.31.
16   Siegel, D. J. (2014).
17   Siegel, D. J. (2014) p.224.
18   Sunderland, M. (2012) p.26.

Chapter Two

1   Golding, K. S. (2008) p.102.
2   Siegel, D. J. (2014) p.12.
3   Sunderland, M. (2012) p.23.
4   Golding, K. S. (2008) p.102.
5   Siegel, D. J. (2014) p.12.
6   Siegel, D. J. (2014) p.80.
7   Golding, K. S. (2008) p.199.
8   Music, G. (2011) p.267.
9   Golding, K. S. (2008) p.216.
10   Golding, K. S. (2008)
11   Archer, C. (1999) *First Steps in Parenting the Child Who Hurts, Tiddlers and Toddlers*. Philadelphia, PA: Jessica Kingsley Publishers and Archer, C. (1999) *Next Steps in Parenting the Child Who Hurts, Tykes and Teens*. London: Jessica Kingsley Publishers.
12   Music, G. (2011) p.19.

Chapter Three

1   Sunderland, M. (2012) p.4.
2   Sunderland, M. (2012) p.1.
3   Hughes, D. and Baylin, J. (2012).
4   Hughes, D. and Baylin, J. (2012) p.7.
5   Hughes, D. and Baylin, J. (2012) p.8.
6   Hughes, D. and Baylin, J. (2012) p.36
7   Siegel, D. J. and Hartzell, M. (2004) *Parenting from the Inside Out*. New York: Tarcher/Penguin.
8   Hughes, D. A. (2006) *Building the Bonds of Attachment: Awakening Love in Deeply Troubled Children*. Northvale, NJ: Aronson.
9   Golding, K. S. (2008) p.166.

10 Selwyn, J., Wijedasa, D. and Meakings, S. (2014) p.9.
11 Hughes, D. and Baylin, J. (2012) p.35.
12 Sunderland, M. (2012) p.14.

Chapter Four

1 Selwyn, J., Wijedasa, D. and Meakings, S. (2014).
2 Selwyn, J., Wijedasa, D. and Meakings, S. (2014) p.187.
3 Selwyn, J., Wijedasa, D. and Meakings, S. (2014) p.188.
4 Selwyn, J., Wijedasa, D. and Meakings, S. (2014) p.260.

Chapter Five

1 Siegel, D. J. (2014) p.3.
2 Keck, G. C. (2009) p.25.
3 Golding, K. S. (2008) p.39.
4 Siegel, D. J. (2014) p.190.
5 Hughes, D. A. (2009) *Attachment Focused Parenting.* New York: W.W. Norton & Company. p.11.
6 Golding, K. S. (2008) p.86.
7 Perry, A. (ed.) (2009) *Teenagers and Attachment.* London: Worth Publishing. p.20.
8 Golding, K. S. (2008).
9 Siegel, D. J. (2014) p.179.
10 Hughes, D. A. (2009) p.11.
11 Golding, K. S. (2008) p.86.
12 Siegel, D. J. (2014) p.185.
13 Perry, A. (ed.) (2009) p.20.
14 Golding, K. S. (2008).
15 Golding, K. S. (2008) p.84.
16 Hughes, D. A. (2009) p.12.
17 Golding, K. S. (2008) p.89.
18 Jernberg, A. M. and Booth, P. B. (2001) *Theraplay: Helping Parents and Children Build Better Relationships Through Attachment-Based Play.'* San Francisco, CA: Jossey-Bass.
19 Siegel, D. J. (2014) p.177.

Chapter Six

1   Erikson, E. H. (1980) *Identity and the Life Cycle*. New York: W.W. Norton & Company.
2   Siegel, D. J. (2014) p.8.
3   Brodinsky, D. M., Schechter, M. D. and Marantz Henig, R. (1993) p.95.
4   Moretti, R. and Holland, R. (2003) *The Journey of Adolescence: Transitions in Self Within the Context of Attachment Relationships*. New York: Guilford Press. p.237.
5   Keck, G. C. (2009) p.35.
6   Siegel, D. J. (2014) p.149.
7   Siegel, D. J. (2014) p.4.
8   Rose, R. and Philpot, T. (2005) *The Child's Own Story: Life Story Work with Traumatized Children*. London: Jessica Kingsley Publishers.

Chapter Seven

1   Brisch, K.L. (2009) 'Attachment and adolescence. The influence of attachment patterns on teenage behaviour.' In A. Perry (ed.) *Teenagers and Attachment Helping Adolescents Engage with Life and Learning*. London: Worth Publishing.
2   Moretti and Holland (2003) p.236.
3   Brisch, K.L. (2009) p.17.
4   Brisch, K.L. (2009) p.20.
5   Brisch, K.L. (2009) p.21.
6   Wolf, T. and Franks, S. (2002) *Get Out of My Life... But First Take Me and Alex into Town*. London: Profile Books. p.226.
7   Siegel, D. J. (2014) p.232.

Chapter Nine

1   Wolf, T. and Franks, S. (2002) p.62.
2   Siegel, D. J. (2014) p.35.
3   Selwyn, J., Wijedasa, D. and Meakings, S. (2014) p.158.
4   Conway, P. (2009) 'Falling in between lines: The effects of unbearable experiences on multi-agency communication in the care system.' *Adoption and Fostering 33*, 1, 18–29.

5   Selwyn, J., Wijedasa, D. and Meakings, S. (2014) p.158.
6   Omer, H. (2004) *Non-Violent Resistance: A New Approach to Violent and Self-Destructive Children.* Cambridge: Cambridge University Press.
7   Cairns, K. (2002) *Attachment, Trauma and Resilience: Therapeutic Caring for Children.* London: BAAF.
8   www.childtrauma.com.
9   Kabat-Zinn, J. (1994) *Wherever You Go, There You Are.* New York: Hyperion.
10   Siegel, D. J. (2014) *Brainstorm.* Australia: Scribe.

INDEX

Eradicating Child
Maltreatment
**Evidence-Based Approaches to
Prevention and Intervention
Across Services**
*Edited by Arnon Bentovim
and Jenny Gray*
Foreword by Harriet Ward

Paperback: £25.00 / $45.00
ISBN: 978 1 84905 449 2
240 pages

Is it possible to overcome the enduring problem of child maltreatment?

In Eradicating Child Maltreatment, leading international figures in the field of child welfare address this enduring and thorny question, setting out a public health approach to prevention. It draws on groundbreaking research and practice on prevention and early intervention from around the globe spanning health, social care, education and criminal justice. Contributors describe what is known about the incidence of child maltreatment, how far we have succeeded in eradicating it, which preventative strategies have been proven to be effective, and offers evidenced recommendations for policy and practice.

Aiming to draw us nearer to the goal of a world free from child maltreatment first articulated by the visionary paediatrician Dr. C. Henry Kempe in 1978, this important book provides new insights for professionals, managers, academics and policymakers across the range of child and family welfare services.

Arnon Bentovim is a Director of Child and Family Training, and a Visiting Professor at Royal Holloway, University of London. He was formerly a Consultant Child and Adolescent Psychiatrist to the

Great Ormond Street Children's Hospital and the Tavistock Clinic. He was also Honorary Senior Lecturer at the Institute of Child Health, University College London. He is co-editor of Safeguarding Children Living with Trauma and Family Violence, published by Jessica Kingsley Publishers.

Jenny Gray OBE is a social work consultant and President of the International Society for the Prevention of Child Abuse and Neglect. From 1995-2012 she was professional adviser to the British government on safeguarding children, firstly in the Department of Health and then in the Department for Education. In this capacity she led policy development on the assessment of children in need, reviews of serious cases and child deaths and the commissioning of safeguarding children research.

Mastering Whole Family Assessment in Social Work Balancing the Needs of Children, Adults and Their Families

Fiona Mainstone

Foreword by Jane Wonnacott

Paperback: £19.99 / $32.95
ISBN: 978 1 84905 240 5
280 pages

How do you keep the whole family in mind when carrying out social work assessment? How do you balance the needs of adults and children? How do you ensure that children's welfare and safety are everyone's priority when families face complex difficulties?

Mastering Whole Family Assessment in Social Work brings together what social workers in adult and children services need to know about assessment across both services. With tools and frameworks that make sense of the interface between adult life difficulties, family problems, parenting capacity and children's needs, this practical guide will help social workers to think across professional and administrative divides. Case studies, practice vignettes, exercises and suggestions for further reading are included throughout the book to help the reader consider the well-being of the whole family when conducting and interpreting assessments.

This guide will help social workers to think holistically and work collaboratively both with each other and with families.

Fiona Mainstone is an independent consultant and educator with many years' experience of social work in local authorities. She contributes to post-graduate programmes at several UK universities and delivers training to managers and practitioners in both adult and children's services. She also practises as a solutions-focused therapist.

**Assessing Disorganized
Attachment Behaviour
in Children**
**An Evidence-Based Model
for Understanding and
Supporting Families**
*Edited by David Shemmings
and Yvonne Shemmings*

Paperback: £22.99 / $32.95
ISBN: 978 1 84905 322 8
240 pages

Assessing Disorganized Attachment Behaviour in Children lays
out an evidence-based model for working with and assessing
children with disorganized attachment and their adult carers:
families whose extreme, erratic and disturbing behaviour can
make them perplexing and frustrating to work with.

The model is designed to identify key indicators and
explanatory mechanisms of child maltreatment: disorganized
attachment in the child, a parent's unresolved loss or trauma,
disconnected and extremely insensitive parenting, and low
parental mentalisation. The book also outlines ways of assessing
children for disorganized attachment and carer capacity, and
proposes interventions.

Accessible and practical, this book is essential reading for child
protection professionals.

David Shemmings is Professor of Child Protection Research in
the School of Social Policy, Sociology and Social Research at the
University of Kent and co-Director of the university's Centre for
Child Protection. He is also visiting professor of Child Protection
Research at Royal Holloway College, University of London. He leads
the Advanced Child Protection stream within the West London
Alliance Post-qualifying Initiative and directs the Assessment of

Disorganised Attachment and Maltreatment (ADAM) Project in over 30 child protection organizations across the UK and Europe.

Yvonne Shemmings is a Continuing Professional Development Specialist and has trained professionals in over 30 child protection organizations. She is a qualified social worker and was also a senior manager. Her work includes the use of attachment theory in practice. Both David and Yvonne have published widely in the fields of child and adult attachment and child protection. Their title, Understanding Disorganized Attachment, is also available from Jessica Kingsley Publishers.